Table of Contents

A Franciscan Tapestry

Life in the Third Order

by

Dr. ant

Although the author and publisher have made every effort to ensure that the information in this book was correct at press time, the author and publisher do not assume and hereby disclaim any liability to any party for any loss, damage, or disruption caused by errors or omissions, whether such errors or omissions result from negligence, accident, or any other cause.

This publication is designed to provide accurate and authoritative information with regard to the subject matter covered. It is sold with the understanding that the publisher is not engaged in rendering professional services. If legal advice or other expert assistance is required, the services of a competent professional should be sought.

The fact that an organization or website is referred to in this work as a citation and/or a potential source of further information does not mean that the author or the publisher endorses the information the organization or website may provide or recommendations it may make.

Please remember that Internet websites listed in this work may have changed or disappeared between when this work was written and when it is read.

A Franciscan Tapestry: Life in the Third Order

Contents

Introduction

The Third Order Regular of St. Francis, often cloaked in the shadows of its more prominent sibling orders, carries within itself a storied past, vibrant contributions to both church and society, and a spiritual legacy that continues to shape lives and futures. The history of this humble yet influential arm of the Franciscan family is a tale marked by fervent faith, relentless service, and unwavering commitment to the ideals set forth by St. Francis of Assisi. Indeed, "Ye are the light of the world. A city that is set on a hill cannot be hid" (Matt. 5:14).

From its inception, the Third Order Regular (TOR) has consumed itself in the struggle to mirror the teachings and vision of its founder, St. Francis. Born in the crucible of 13th-century Italy, where faith and culture battled for supremacy, this Order emerged as a beacon for laypeople seeking a deeper, more committed life within the secular world. Echoing the Gospel of St. Luke, "The kingdom of God is within you" (Luke 17:21), the TOR thrived on the conviction that holiness and spiritual fervor could be pursued steadfastly outside the cloister. Thus, it invited and still invites its members to walk a path of devotion intertwined with the mundane, urging each person to transform ordinary life into an extraordinary pilgrimage.

Embodying the spirit of St. Francis, the Third Order Regular placed its trust in embracing a life of poverty, chastity, and obedience, while simultaneously fostering active engagement in the community. These principles heralded a new kind of religious life that embraced the world rather than retreating from it entirely. This bold vision made the TOR a pivotal force in spreading the Franciscan charism, not merely as a relic of monastic asceticism but as a dynamic domain for lay involvement and sanctification of everyday life. The words of the Holy Scripture, "For where your treasure is, there will your heart be also" (Matt. 6:21), resounded in the hearts of these early members as they endeavored to dedicate their lives to the service of God and humanity.

The contributions of the Third Order Regular extend well beyond the walls of the church, touching various aspects of society through their rich tradition of service. They have been vanguards of evangelization, educators par excellence, and champions of social justice. Their efforts straddle the sacred and the secular, ensuring that every soul they encounter sees Christ in their actions. The ethos of St. Francis, harmonizing simplicity with profound compassion, permeates their numerous ventures around the globe. These acts of service resonate deeply with the biblical charge, "Bear ye one another's burdens, and so fulfil the law of Christ" (Gal. 6:2).

The TOR's illustrious history is punctuated by the lives of countless saints and blessed figures who have tread this humble path with piety and perseverance. From St. Elizabeth of Hungary to Blessed Angela of Foligno, their lives are a testimony to the transformative power of faith and devotion. Their stories are interwoven with divine encounters, acts of charity, and an insatiable thirst for God's love. These saints serve as luminous examples to the faithful, embodying the virtues of the Franciscan way and demonstrating how ordinary lives can be transfigured into instruments of divine grace.

Within the academic sphere, the Third Order Regular has also carved a niche for itself, particularly through institutions like the Franciscan University of Steubenville. Founded on the principles of faith, reason, and service, such institutions have become bastions of Catholic education, integrally linking intellectual pursuit with spiritual growth. They strive to cultivate disciples of Christ who are well-prepared to meet the world's challenges armed with wisdom, virtue, and integrity. This educational mission is inspired by the Pauline exhortation, "And be not conformed to this world: but be ye transformed by the renewing of your mind" (Rom. 12:2).

As we journey through the chapters of this book, the manifold dimensions of the TOR's life and legacy will unfold before us. The reader will be invited to delve into their foundational spirituality, their unwavering commitment to the church and the broader world, and the theological and literary contributions they have made over centuries. The narrative will not just recount historical milestones but will also illuminate the enduring, vibrant presence of the Third Order Regular in the contemporary era, showcasing how their mission continues to resonate today.

In a world fraught with turmoil and distractions, the enduring message of the Third Order Regular offers a countercultural witness grounded in contemplation and action. Their path invites all to find sacredness in simplicity, to seek holiness in the heart of community life, and to uplift the downtrodden with unwavering compassion. With each subsequent chapter, may we be inspired by their profound journey and indelible contributions, echoing the scripture, "Blessed are the peacemakers: for they shall be called the children of God" (Matt. 5:9). Through this exploration, may we glean insights into living a life that embodies the humility, devotion, and charity championed by Saint Francis and his spiritual descendants.

Therefore, let us open our hearts and minds as we commence this exploration into the venerable tradition of the Third Order Regular. Through the stories, teachings, and enduring legacy of these remarkable men and women, may we find our own lives enriched and our spirits emboldened to walk the path of holiness with renewed vigor and dedication.

Chapter 1: The Founding of the Third Order

In the days when the whispers of the Lord were carried by the wind through the valleys of Umbria, a fervent desire to live the Gospel more fully took root in the hearts of both laymen and clerics. Guided by the luminous vision of St. Francis of Assisi, whose name gleams like a torch in the annals of holy men, they yearned for a path that transcended worldly attachments yet did not retreat into the cloistered life. This movement, blessed by divine providence, culminated in the founding of the Third Order—an order neither anchored in the secular world nor bound by the confines of the monastery, but rather one that sanctified daily living through commitment to humility, poverty, and charity. Imbued with the words of Christ, who said, "He that hath two coats, let him impart to him that hath none" (Luke 3:11), the Third Order embraced those teachings with a fervor that illuminated their spirits. Thus began their sacred journey, a pilgrimage of both mind and soul, unfolding a radiant chapter in the tapestry of the Church.

Origins and Early History

The dawn of the Third Order's illustrious journey begins in a time of spiritual renaissance, a period marred by both sanctity and strife. Enrooted deeply in the fertile ground of the medieval church, its origins can be traced back to a desire to live out the gospel in an authentic and community-centered way. The genesis was not marked by grand proclamations or celestial phenomena; rather, it was born out of humble, earnest yearnings to follow in the footsteps of Saint Francis of Assisi.

Saint Francis of Assisi, whose own transformation from wealth to a life of poverty and devotion still echoes through the annals of history, offered a beacon of light to laymen and laywomen restless with their secular existence. It was a time when the church grappled with both its spiritual mission and temporal power—an era ripe for reform and renewed zeal. Saint Francis' charisma and dedication inspired a multitude beyond the cloistered walls of monasteries and convents, kindling a new form of communal spiritual commitment.

This burgeoning community emerged not from the ordained halls of clergy but rather from the heart of ordinary people— merchants, farmers, and artisans—who yearned to pursue a path of sanctity within the framework of their daily lives. This, the Third Order, or Tertiaries as they were affectionately called, sought to bridge the divide between the sacred and the secular. They aspired to embody the divine virtues of humility, simplicity, and charity, transcending the traditional confines of religious life.

In 1221, Saint Francis drafted a preliminary rule for what was to become the Third Order, distinct from the friars and nuns yet equally committed to living out the gospel. This rule was neither oppressive nor burdensome; it was a simple guide encouraging daily prayer, penitential observation, and works of mercy. Drawn from Saint Paul's wisdom, it was a call, "Let love be without dissimulation. Abhor that which is evil; cleave to that which is good" (Rom. 12:9). And thus, the foundation stones were set.

Over time, these laymen and laywomen formed small communities, often in villages and towns that resonated with the Franciscan ethos. They helped tend to the sick, feed the hungry, and clothe the poor, becoming a living testament to the gospel's call for charity. The testimonies of their deeds grew, spreading through whispered tales and written word, instilling a burgeoning respect and admiration. Their existence was not one of grandiose piety but a sincere, palpable manifestation of Christ's teachings.

As the order grew, so did the need for greater structure and guidance. The Third Order became more formalized, receiving papal acknowledgment and ecclesiastical support. The 1247 papal letter of Pope Innocent IV, "Cum de Quibusdam," recognized the rules established by Saint Francis and confirmed the legitimacy of the lay brotherhood. It was a monumental step, ensuring they were entwined with the broader church's mission without losing their unique identity as a lay congregation dedicated to living out Franciscan virtues.

Amidst the ecclesiastical recognition, the Tertiaries maintained their humble beginnings' essence. They revered Saint Francis not just as a figurehead but as a spiritual father whose principles were to be lived daily. "Blessed are the meek: for they shall inherit the earth" (Matt. 5:5) was not just a verse for contemplation but a call to action, inspiring them to forge their path with quiet strength and unwavering faith.

These communities continued to grow and solidify their presence, particularly in Italy and later expanding throughout Europe. The tumultuous climate of the Middle Ages, marked by wars, plagues, and political upheavals, only seemed to strengthen the resolve of the Third Order. They became embodiments of steadfast faith and charity amid societal chaos, often the very hands and feet of Christ in their beleaguered communities.

Moreover, the Third Order's influence began to permeate other societal facets beyond mere spiritual endeavours. Their commitment to education, healthcare, and social justice laid the groundwork for future generations. Hospitals, schools, and charitable institutions often found their genesis in the altruistic hearts of these Franciscan laypersons. They sought to heal not only the soul but the body and mind, recognizing the holistic nature of human need.

As time unfurled, the order began to welcome more members from different walks of life. The inclusivity of the Third Order was an immense drawcard. Rich and poor, young and old, married and single—all found a place within this spiritual tapestry. This melange of individuals brought diverse talents and skills, further enriching the order's mission and outreach. The Third Order became a microcosm of the Christian ideal—a community where every limb of the body of Christ was valued and every talent utilized for the greater good.

Even as it swelled in numbers, the Third Order remained unyieldingly committed to its founding principles. It wasn't merely about numerical growth but depth of spiritual life and authentic living. The Tertiaries continually returned to Saint Francis' teachings, leading lives that bore witness to a gospel unadulterated by time or circumstance. "And be ye kind one to another, tenderhearted, forgiving one another, even as God for

Christ's sake hath forgiven you" (Eph. 4:32) served as a lodestar in their interactions, both within and beyond their communities.

In the span of its early history, the Third Order passed through numerous trials and triumphs, each chapter adding to its rich narrative. It was not a tale of unceasing prosperity nor unmitigated hardship but a nuanced tapestry woven with threads of divine grace and human perseverance. The members understood that their vocation was not merely to mirror religious life but to transform secular existence into a living testament of God's love and mercy.

The stories of their lives, chronicles of their unwavering devotion, and the changing landscapes of their missions form a vibrant mosaic that continued to inspire subsequent generations. In these humble beginnings lay the seeds of a dazzling legacy—a testament to what happens when ordinary men and women choose to live extraordinary lives fueled by faith. "For where your treasure is, there will your heart be also" (Matt. 6:21); indeed, their hearts remained entirely devoted to God's love and service.

As this chapter in history closed, it became evident that the phenomenon of the Third Order transcended a mere religious movement. It became an incarnational spirituality that infused everyday life with an enduring, divine purpose. Their humble beginnings were but the dawn of a luminous journey that would continue to shine forth Christ's love in myriad ways, transforming the world one act of charity at a time.

St. Francis of Assisi and His Vision

As we delve into the heart of the Third Order's founding, we must turn our gaze toward the very soul who envisioned it: St. Francis of Assisi. His journey from a life of affluent ease to one of radical poverty and profound spirituality forms the bedrock upon which the Third Order rests. St. Francis' vision was not just an ethereal dream, but a powerful calling that crystallized into a movement encompassing laity and clergy alike.

Upon his spiritual awakening, St. Francis wholly abandoned his former pursuits. He began to live a life modeled after Christ, marked by humility, service, and ecstatic communion with God's creation. "Take nothing for your journey," Jesus instructed His disciples, "neither staves, nor scrip, neither bread, neither money" (Luke 9:3), and in this vein, St. Francis and his followers embraced absolute poverty. Clad in simple robes and devoid of earthly possessions, they preached the Gospel through their very existence, embodying Christ's teachings in every action.

Francis disdained material wealth, seeing it as a barrier between the soul and God. His life was a testament to the Beatitudes, particularly: "Blessed are the poor in spirit: for theirs is the kingdom of heaven" (Matt. 5:3). Yet, his vision transcended mere asceticism. Francis perceived all of creation as a magnificent symphony of divine love, each element singing praise to the Creator. He addressed even the lowliest creatures as brothers and sisters, affirming the sacred interconnectedness of all life.

His understanding of brotherhood was not limited to the natural world but extended to human society in a revolutionary way. In St. Francis' eyes, the Christian community was not to be divided by distinctions of class, vocation, or status. This was the germination of the Third Order, a fellowship where laypeople could live out Franciscan spirituality while remaining in their secular lives. Deeply moved by Jesus' call to love one's neighbor, St. Francis envisioned a world knitted together by bonds of compassion, kindness, and mutual aid.

Francis' vision was crystallized in his establishment of three orders. The First Order, for men, and the Second Order, for women, were cloistered and dedicated to monastic life. However, the genius of St. Francis lay in his creation of the Third Order. This was a space where laypeople—merchants, farmers, mothers, fathers—could imbue their daily activities with spiritual purpose, without cloister walls separating them from the world.

Thus, the Third Order Regular Franciscans were born, a testament to St. Francis' radical inclusivity. It allowed countless men and women to partake in the Franciscan charism—without renouncing their familial or social obligations. Herein lies a transformative vision: sanctity is not confined within monasteries but blooms through the common paths of daily life. For St. Francis, the sacred was not distant but woven into the fabric of everyday existence.

Central to the ethos of the Third Order is the profound simplicity and joyous spirit of their founder. St. Francis embraced suffering and joy with equal fervor, seeing both as pathways to divine intimacy. His joyful song, "The Canticle of the Creatures," exudes a rapture for God's creation that has inspired generations. Such irrepressible joy, combined with an unwavering commitment to poverty, humility, and charity, became the hallmark of the Third Order.

The vision of St. Francis, encompassing both his deep love for creation and his radical embrace of poverty, shaped the ethos of the Third Order Regular Franciscans. He taught that one could live a fully spiritual life while being fully immersed in the world, an idea that was both revolutionary and profoundly liberating. This integrated life of action and contemplation drew many to the Third Order, strengthening the Church and enriching global communities through the centuries.

In his relentless pursuit of divine love, St. Francis often retreated to solitude, yet his heart remained bound by compassion to the world's pain. He exemplified the Apostolic advice, "Bear ye one another's burdens, and so fulfill the law of Christ" (Galatians 6:2). The inception of the Third Order embodied this apostolic spirit—offering a way of life where laypeople could address societal needs while walking the path of righteousness.

The practical outworking of St. Francis' vision saw the Third Order members engaging in various social missions. They provided charity to the poor, nursed the sick, and acted as mediators in conflicts. Their service continued to expand globally, each act of kindness a testament to the enduring influence of their founder's vision. As St. Francis professed, it is in giving that we receive, and this selfless service has garnered heavenly treasures and widespread respect for the Third Order.

To truly appreciate the scope of St. Francis' vision for the Third Order, one must delve into its foundational statutes. Given the simple rule set by Francis, the members were to live in their homes, follow their trade, and yet dedicate themselves to the principles of prayer, penance, and works of mercy. These statutes reflect his all-encompassing vision, urging members toward constant spiritual growth while remaining active participants in their communities.

St. Francis' approach remained ever dynamic, ready to adapt to God's calling. Just as he mended the physical church of San

Damiano, he sought to mend the spiritual fabric of society. Each Third Order member, in carrying this vision forward, becomes a living stone in the spiritual edifice St. Francis aspired to build. By committing to the principles of peace, love, and service, they continue to restore and renew the world.

Ultimately, St. Francis of Assisi's vision for the Third Order encompasses a radical reorientation of life toward divine love and service. It is a journey of inward transformation manifesting outwardly in acts of kindness and social justice. With tender humility and unwavering dedication, Francis' followers—the Third Order Regular Franciscans—embody an enduring legacy that continues to inspire the hearts and minds of those who seek to live out the Gospel in its fullness.

Chapter 2: Spirituality of the Third Order Regular

The spirituality of the Third Order Regular is a radiant tapestry woven from the threads of humble servitude and divine reverence, following the luminous example of St. Francis of Assisi. This spiritual path beckons its followers to embrace the sacred mysteries of Jesus Christ with hearts rooted in simplicity and ardor. In the Gospel's light, they seek to manifest the virtues of the Beatitudes, living in communities that reflect the Kingdom of Heaven on earth. "Blessed are the poor in spirit: for theirs is the kingdom of heaven" (Matt. 5:3). The daily practices of prayer, penance, and acts of charity form the lifeblood of their devout existence, transforming the mundane into profound expressions of God's love. Driven by a fervent commitment to the evangelical counsels—poverty, chastity, and obedience—they endeavor to become living vessels of peace and goodwill, offering their lives as a testament to the enduring power of faith and communal harmony.

Franciscan Approach to Jesus

The Franciscan approach to Jesus is an intimate and Christ-centric spirituality, deeply embedded in the lives and practices of the Third Order Regular. It is an approach rooted in love, humility, and a profound sense of connection with the divine. St. Francis of Assisi, the heart and soul of the Franciscan charism, found his fundamental inspiration in the life and teachings of Jesus Christ, particularly emphasizing the Incarnation and the Passion. Through the lens of Franciscan spirituality, Jesus is seen not just as the Savior and Redeemer but as a divine brother who shares in our humanity.

One central aspect of this approach is the embrace of Jesus' humanity. St. Francis was moved by the humble birth of Jesus in a manger, an event that to him symbolized the profound humility and vulnerability of God. The nativity scene, therefore, becomes a powerful representation of God's solidarity with humankind, offering a model of simplicity and poverty. This aspect of Franciscan spirituality invites the faithful to live humbly and to serve others, especially the poor and marginalized, emulating the Christ child who came into the world in a state of poverty.

Moreover, the Passion of Christ holds a place of preeminence in the Franciscan approach. St. Francis was known for his intense meditation on the sufferings of Jesus, leading to profound mystical experiences, including the reception of the stigmata. This focus on the Passion underscores the Franciscan belief in the transformative power of suffering when united with Christ's own. The Crucified One is thus a profound symbol of divine love and redemption, calling all Franciscans to a deeper conversion and imitation of Christ's self-sacrificial love. "But God commendeth his love toward us, in that, while we were yet sinners, Christ died for us" (Rom. 5:8).

This spirituality is also profoundly incarnational. Franciscans are called to see and experience Jesus in the everyday realities of life, recognizing His presence in all creation. This is rooted in the theological concept of the primacy of Christ, which posits that the Incarnation was part of God's original plan, irrespective of the fall of man. Hence, Jesus is seen as the ultimate revelation of God's love and intention for creation, calling the faithful to a life of gratitude and reverence for all that exists. "For by him were all things created, that are in heaven, and that are in earth, visible and invisible" (Col. 1:16).

Prayer, contemplation, and action are harmoniously intertwined in the Franciscan approach to Jesus. The life of prayer is not an escape from the world, but rather a deep engagement with it through the eyes of Christ. Franciscan prayer often takes the form of quiet contemplation, gazing upon the face of Jesus in the

Eucharist, Scripture, and in the faces of brothers and sisters. This contemplative gaze fosters a spirit of compassion and mercy, inspiring acts of charity and justice.

Poverty and joy, paradoxically, go hand in hand in the Franciscan vision of following Jesus. The evangelical counsel of poverty is not only a renunciation of material wealth but also an embrace of spiritual richness in Christ. St. Francis called his followers to "Lady Poverty," viewing it as a path to true joy and freedom. This voluntary poverty is a witness to the sufficiency of God's grace and the abundance found in living a life modeled after Jesus, who "though he was rich, yet for your sakes he became poor, that ye through his poverty might be rich" (2 Cor. 8:9).

Community life in the Third Order Regular is another cornerstone of their approach to Jesus. Following the example of the early Christian community and inspired by Jesus' life with His disciples, Franciscans live out their faith in communal settings. This communal life is characterized by shared prayer, mutual support, and collective mission, reflecting the very nature of the Church as the Body of Christ. It is within this community that individual paths to holiness are nurtured and sustained.

The Franciscan devotion to the Holy Eucharist is profound and all-encompassing. The Eucharist is viewed as the living presence of Christ, a mystical union with the divine that sustains and transforms the believer. This devotion is not confined to the act of receiving Communion but extends to Eucharistic adoration and a deep reverence for the sacrament as the source and summit of Christian life. "This is my body, which is broken for you: this do in remembrance of me" (1 Cor. 11:24).

In preaching and mission, the Franciscan approach to Jesus emphasizes the embodiment of the Gospel in action and word. Preaching is not merely about verbal proclamation but is made credible through a life that mirrors the teachings of Christ. St. Francis' exhortation to "Preach the Gospel at all times; when necessary, use words," encapsulates this holistic understanding of evangelization. This approach calls Franciscans to live as witnesses of Christ's love, compassion, and justice in every aspect of their lives.

Furthermore, the Franciscan approach to Jesus is deeply Marian. St. Francis' devotion to Mary, Mother of Jesus, shows the intimate link between the two hearts. Mary is seen as the first disciple, the Theotokos who brought Jesus into the world through her fiat. Her Magnificat becomes the canticle of the poor and the joyful song of the redeemed. Franciscans look to Mary as a model of faith, humility, and discipleship, inspiring them to a deeper devotion to Jesus through her example. "And Mary said, Behold the handmaid of the Lord; be it unto me according to thy word" (Luke 1:38).

In addition, the works of mercy are fundamental to the Franciscan way. Inspired by Jesus' parables and teachings, they seek to embody the corporal and spiritual works of mercy, bringing healing, comfort, and hope to those in need. The practice of these works is not a mere social action but a tangible expression of Christ's love. It is an incarnate spirituality that sees Jesus in the least of our brothers and sisters, heeding His words, "Inasmuch as ye have done it unto one of the least of these my brethren, ye have done it unto me" (Matt. 25:40).

Finally, the Franciscan approach to Jesus invites a continual conversion of heart, mind, and spirit. This ongoing metanoia is reflective of Jesus' call to repentance and renewal. It is a lifelong journey of becoming more like Jesus, marked by moments of grace, struggle, and transformation. This process is deeply personal yet communal, as each member of the Third Order Regular supports one another in the pilgrimage towards holiness. "Being confident of this very thing, that he which hath begun a good work in you will perform it until the day of Jesus Christ" (Phil. 1:6).

In essence, the Franciscan approach to Jesus is a dynamic and relational spirituality, deeply centered on Christ's life and love. It offers a pathway of simplicity, humility, and joy, calling the faithful to follow in the footsteps

Daily Life and Practices

The daily life and practices of the Third Order Regular Franciscans are steeped in simplicity, humility, and devotion, reflecting the profound spiritual legacy of St. Francis of Assisi. Rooted in the Rule of Life given by St. Francis, members of the Third Order seek to emulate Christ in all aspects of their lives, adopting a path of poverty, chastity, and obedience. This spiritual journey begins with the Liturgy of the Hours, a series of prayers that mark the rhythm of the day—morning, midday, evening, and night, drawing the faithful ever closer to God.

"Pray without ceasing," admonishes the Apostle Paul (1 Thess. 5:17). In keeping with this exhortation, the life of a Third Order Regular is punctuated by frequent prayer and reflection. The day often starts before dawn, with Lauds or Morning Prayer, exuding a spirit of gratitude for the new day granted by the Creator. This is followed by a time of personal meditation and the Holy Eucharist, where members find their spiritual sustenance in the blessed sacrament, re-living the mystery of Christ's sacrifice.

Their prayers are not confined to formal rituals. Franciscans are encouraged to practice "contemplative action," weaving prayer into the fabric of their daily tasks. Whether they are tending to a garden, teaching a class, or serving the poor, every activity is an offering to God. Their work becomes an extension of their prayer, exemplifying the commandment, "And whatsoever ye do, do it heartily, as to the Lord, and not unto men" (Col. 3:23).

In the spirit of communal living, the Third Order Regular Franciscans also gather for meals, which are simple and shared. These gatherings are more than just nourishment for the body; they are occasions for fellowship, where the bonds of brotherhood and sisterhood are strengthened. Each meal, often preceded and followed by prayers of thanksgiving, reinforces their collective commitment to live in harmony and mutual support.

Additionally, silence plays a critical role in their spiritual formation. Each day includes periods of silence, especially after Compline or Night Prayer, to meditate on the word of God and examine their conscience. The night closes with a prayer of protection and peace: "I will both lay me down in peace, and sleep: For thou, Lord, only makest me dwell in safety" (Ps. 4:8).

The communal spirit is further nurtured through regular chapter meetings, a tradition where all members come together to discuss spiritual matters, community issues, and the ongoing discernment of their mission. Such gatherings are occasions of cherished fraternal love and mutual edification, akin to the early

Christian communities described in Acts: "And all that believed were together, and had all things common" (Acts 2:44).

In their apostolic endeavors, Third Order Franciscans are often seen in educational institutions, hospitals, and social service centers. Their ministries reflect the holistic approach of caring for both body and soul. Education, seen as an act of love and a path to liberation, is a significant domain wherein they leave a lasting impact, enlightening minds while nurturing spirits in the light of Gospel values.

Their days are not without leisure and recreation, albeit in a manner consistent with their vows. Simplicity in recreation helps keep them grounded and in touch with one another and with nature. It is not unusual to find them walking in the woods, tending to gardens, or engaging in modest artistic pursuits, each activity graced with the spirit of "holy leisure" that St. Francis himself embraced.

Moreover, their life is characterized by acts of penance. Observing Fridays as days of fasting and abstinence, they remember the passion of Christ, mortifying their flesh to elevate their spirit. Penances are community-oriented and decided collectively, yet each member has the freedom to undertake additional personal sacrifices as moved by the Spirit.

The rhythm of Third Order life is also marked by seasons of special devotion. Advent and Lent are observed with heightened prayer, fasting, and almsgiving, preparing the heart for the profound mysteries of Incarnation and Redemption. During these periods, they engage more deeply in acts of charity, reaching out to the marginalized in society, thus embodying Christ's love and compassion.

The embrace of poverty is not merely a renunciation of material wealth but an attitude of complete reliance on God's providence. St. Francis's admonition to "own nothing of your own" permeates their lives. Thus, their possessions are meager and held in common, reinforcing a communal identity over an individual one. It is a continual reminder of Jesus' words, "Lay not up for yourselves treasures upon earth, where moth and rust doth corrupt" (Matt. 6:19).

Chastity, both in its literal and spiritual dimensions, is a crucial aspect of their daily practice. It is not simply celibacy but a call to purity of heart, focusing entirely on God's love. Their interactions are suffused with charity and simplicity, treating every person as a manifestation of Christ, fostering an environment where fraternal love flourishes untainted by selfish desires.

Obedience, the cornerstone of their vows, transcends mere compliance with rules. It is an active, joyful submission to God's will, as discerned through their superiors and the community. This obedience fosters unity and purpose, ensuring that each action aligns with their collective mission and the transformative power of the Gospel.

The daily life of the Third Order Regular Franciscans is replete with opportunities for sanctification, shaped by a routine that continually draws them closer to God and neighbor. Their practices, born from the profound spiritual insights of St. Francis, offer a living testament to a life entirely surrendered to divine providence and love. In their humble, joyful witness, they bring to life the vision of a Gospel-centered life, teaching by example the transformative power of faith.

Chapter 3: Contributions to the Church

From the annals of history, the Third Order Regular Franciscans have stood as luminous beacons of faith and service, ever dedicated to the Church. Their unparalleled commitment to evangelization and missionary work has sown seeds of faith across distant lands, resonating with the Great Commission, "Go ye therefore, and teach all nations" (Matt. 28:19). Through skillful educational initiatives, they've uplifted countless souls, infusing wisdom with divine love, and knitting communities closer to the heart of Christ. These endeavors, both grand and humble, reflect the enduring spirit of St. Francis, manifesting the Kingdom of God on earth. "And whatsoever ye do, do it heartily, as to the Lord, and not unto men" (Col. 3:23), guiding every action towards a higher purpose. In their fervent work, the Third Order Regular Franciscans have not merely contributed to the Church—they have become indispensable threads in its sacred tapestry, embodying a legacy of spiritual fortitude and transformative grace.

Evangelization and Missionary Work

The Franciscan Third Order Regular has, through the centuries, become a beacon of evangelical zeal and missionary fervor. Rooted in the teachings of St. Francis of Assisi, whose desire was to spread the Gospel to the ends of the earth, these dedicated members have carried forth the light of Christ into the darkest corners of the world. Their commitment to evangelization and missionary work has borne fruit across continents, transforming both the landscape of faith and the lives of countless individuals.

One of the most remarkable aspects of the Third Order's evangelistic efforts is their humility and simplicity. Emulating the life of Christ, Franciscans have often chosen to dwell among the poorest and most marginalized of society. Their approach to spreading the Gospel has not been through grandiose sermons or opulent cathedrals, but through living examples of Christ's love and compassion. In line with the words of our Lord, "Go ye into all the world, and preach the gospel to every creature" (Mark 16:15), they have ventured into places where others might not dare to tread.

The Third Order's evangelization strategy can be described as incarnational. They have immersed themselves in the cultures and communities they seek to evangelize. Unlike other missionary endeavors that might impose a foreign identity upon a culture, Franciscan missionaries work to understand and engage with the local customs, finding ways to integrate the Gospel message within that context. This practice has not only respected the dignity of the people but has also made the message of Christ more accessible and understandable.

This incarnational approach extends to their methods of teaching and preaching. It is often said that Franciscans preach the Gospel always, but only use words when necessary. The life of a Franciscan missionary is itself a profound sermon. Through acts of charity, healthcare, education, and environmental stewardship, they communicate the love of Christ. Mirroring the Scriptural direction, "Let your light so shine before men, that they may see your good works, and glorify your Father which is in heaven" (Matt. 5:16), their lives become beacons of divine light.

Education has formed a critical part of their evangelistic mission. By establishing schools and universities, Franciscans have not only imparted knowledge but also instilled values of faith, hope, and charity. These educational institutions have become the breeding ground for future leaders who carry forward the Gospel's message into various facets of societal life. Yet, their contribution has never been just about intellectual enrichment; it has been deeply tied to spiritual formation, grounding students in the rich soil of Franciscan spirituality.

The Franciscan missionaries' commitment to healthcare has also played a pivotal role in their evangelistic efforts. Hospitals and clinics established by the order serve as sanctuaries for the sick and suffering, places where the healing hands of Christ are made manifest. Medical missions often open doors that traditional evangelization methods might struggle to unlock, reaching out to the physical needs before addressing the spiritual ones. Their care echoes the Scriptural mandate, "Heal the sick, cleanse the lepers, raise the dead, cast out devils: freely ye have received, freely give" (Matt. 10:8).

Over time, their missions have stretched from the crowded streets of medieval Europe to the remote jungles of South America, from the sun-scorched landscapes of Africa to the bustling cities of Asia. Each new mission field presents distinct challenges, yet the Third Order Franciscans adapt with creativity and resilience, guided always by the Spirit. This dynamic adaptability is rooted in the Franciscan vow of poverty, which emphasizes frugality and inventiveness, often using scarce resources to achieve great things for God's kingdom.

The story of the Third Order's missionary work is also one of martyrs and saints. Many have faced persecution and even death in their quest to spread the Gospel. Their sacrifices echo the profound message of Christ's own passion, reinforcing the eternal truth that "Greater love hath no man than this, that a man lay down his life for his friends" (John 15:13). These martyrdoms serve as a testament to their deep commitment and unwavering faith, inspiring future generations to take up the mantle of evangelization with the same fervor and courage.

Moreover, the Third Order's missionary endeavors have included significant efforts in interfaith dialogue and cooperation. In regions where they encountered religious diversity, they have sought common ground, fostering understanding and mutual respect. Their work does not seek to dominate but to coexist with other faith traditions, creating avenues for peaceful coexistence and joint efforts in social justice and humanitarian campaigns. This spirit of dialogue is deeply rooted in Franciscan values and in the Gospel's call for love and unity, "A new commandment I give unto you, That ye love one another; as I have loved you, that ye also love one another" (John 13:34).

Sustainability and environmental stewardship have also become integral components of their evangelistic mission. By promoting care for creation, they have connected the hearts of the people with the Creator, emphasizing that the stewardship of the earth is a sacred duty. This mission aligns with St. Francis himself, the patron saint of ecology, who saw all creation as a reflection of God's glory. With a deep sense of interconnectedness, they teach that preserving our planet is both an act of faith and a testament to our love for future generations.

One can't overlook the contribution of the Third Order's many missionary outposts and residences, which stand as enduring symbols of their unwavering commitment and service. These establishments, often built with the simplest of resources, become spiritual oases in foreign lands, centers of community life, prayer, and service. They offer not only refuge to the weary traveler but also hospitality and love to the stranger, fulfilling the commandment to love thy neighbor as thyself (Matt. 22:39).

The lessons drawn from their missions resonate through generations, inspiring not just Franciscans but all who seek to live out the Gospel. Their work has not just been about conversion in the traditional sense but about transformation—bringing hope, restoring dignity, and building communities grounded in the love of Christ. Echoing the Apostle Paul, they "become all things to all men, that [they] might by all means save some" (1 Cor. 9:22).

In summary, the evangelization and missionary work of the Third Order Regular Franciscans remains a testament to their faith, resilience, and unwavering commitment to Christ's Great Commission. Their story continues to unfold, written in acts of love, sacrifice, and the persistent hope of the Kingdom come.

From their humble beginnings to their global impact, their contributions to evangelization are monumental and continue to shape the Church's mission in a rapidly changing world.

Educational Initiatives

The roots of the educational initiatives within the Third Order Regular of the Franciscans are deep and manifold, founded upon the charism of St. Francis of Assisi. His vision of humble service, combined with an unyielding thirst for knowledge, has long been a guiding light in the Order's efforts to enlighten minds and uplift souls. "The fear of the Lord is the beginning of wisdom: and the knowledge of the holy is understanding" (Prov. 9:10), and thus the Franciscans have sought to share this understanding through various educational ventures.

Throughout generations, the Third Order Regular (TOR) has dedicated itself to cultivating a legacy of intellectual and spiritual formation. They established schools, universities, and learning centers across continents, each institution aimed at nourishing the spirit and mind in tandem. These efforts reflect not just an academic pursuit, but one that is intrinsically linked to the spiritual growth of individuals, fostering communities built upon Franciscan values of humility, charity, and love.

In Europe, especially during the medieval period, the TOR played a pivotal role in the foundation of schools that catered to the children of both the elite and the common folk. Their educational philosophy was, and remains, one of inclusivity and accessibility. The Order believed that education should not be a privilege reserved for the few but a right available to all. Hence, they worked diligently to ensure that even the poorest could receive a quality education that nurtured both their intellect and faith.

Endeavors began humbly with parish schools where basic literacy, numeracy, and religious education were imparted. Over time, the vision expanded. Monastic schools attached to Franciscan friaries blossomed into larger institutions, becoming places where theological, philosophical, and classical studies flourished. Such efforts were in line with the admonition of St. Paul: "Study to shew thyself approved unto God, a workman that needeth not to be ashamed, rightly dividing the word of truth" (2 Tim. 2:15).

The post-Reformation period saw an even broader scope of Franciscan educational initiatives, particularly as the Order sought new ways to engage and convert souls through education. This era brought about the establishment of some of the most revered institutions in the Catholic educational tradition, including several universities that combined rigorous academic programs with profound spiritual life, such as the esteemed Franciscan University of Steubenville.

Within these hallowed halls, the interplay between faith and reason is celebrated and nurtured, ensuring that graduates are not just well-versed in their academic disciplines, but also deeply rooted in their spiritual heritage. The Franciscan approach to education emphasizes the integration of moral values with intellectual rigor, reflecting the words of Proverbs: "Train up a child in the way he should go: and when he is old, he will not depart from it" (Prov. 22:6).

In the realm of pedagogy, the TOR has been innovative and forward-thinking. They pioneer educational methods and curricula that balance classical teachings with contemporary needs. Franciscan educators place a heavy emphasis on experiential learning, community service, and a holistic approach to student development. These educational practices are designed to cultivate not merely scholars, but whole persons who are prepared to lead lives of service and compassion, embodying Christ's teaching: "For even the Son of man came not to be ministered unto, but to minister, and to give his life a ransom for many" (Mark 10:45).

Furthermore, the TOR championed the education of women at times when such opportunities were scant. They supported and established numerous convent schools where young women could receive an education equal to that offered to their male counterparts. Their commitment to the empowerment of women through education is a testament to their progressive ideals and dedication to social equity.

The Franciscan educational mission has never been confined to the physical domain of schools and universities. It extends to the creation of publications, theological treatises, and other written works that disseminate knowledge far and wide. Many within the Order have contributed significantly to theological literature, ensuring that the treasures of their spiritual insights are shared with Christian communities worldwide.

In the mission lands, the Third Order Regular has continued this tradition of educational outreach. From the Americas to Asia and Africa, they established missions where education is a cornerstone of their evangelical work. These mission schools often serve as beacons of hope in regions afflicted by poverty and conflict, providing not only academic education but a sense of stability and spiritual solace.

In recent times, the TOR has embraced the digital age, recognizing the transformative power of technology in education. They have developed online courses, virtual classrooms, and digital libraries that make Franciscan education accessible to a global audience. This modern approach ensures that the Franciscan educational legacy continues to evolve and reach hearts and minds across the world.

Yet, no matter how advanced the methods or widespread the outreach, the core of Franciscan educational initiatives has always remained steadfast: to educate in the love and knowledge of Christ. This dual commitment to intellectual and spiritual development, akin to two sides of the same coin, forms the bedrock of their legacy. St. Paul's exhortation articulates this beautifully: "And be not conformed to this world: but be ye transformed by the renewing of your mind, that ye may prove what is that good, and acceptable, and perfect, will of God" (Rom. 12:2).

The impact of these educational initiatives stretches far beyond the walls of classrooms and into the very fabric of society. Alumni of Franciscan institutions carry forth ideals of service, integrity, and compassion, making significant contributions to various fields while embodying the Franciscan spirit. Thus, the efforts of the Third Order Regular in education have not only illuminated individual minds but have also contributed to the greater good of humanity.

As we reflect upon these endeavors, it becomes evident that the Franciscan commitment to education is more than an academic pursuit; it is a divine calling, a sacred duty carried out with humility and love. The Third Order Regular Franciscans have woven a rich tapestry of educational excellence that continues to inspire and guide souls towards the eternal light of wisdom and faith.

Chapter 4: Contributions to the World

The legacy of the Third Order Regular of St. Francis resounds across the realms of social justice, charity, and environmental stewardship, echoing the clarion call of Christ to "love thy neighbor as thyself" (Matt. 22:39). Through actions imbued with a piercing compassion, these Franciscans constructed a bulwark of hope for the poor and marginalized, embodying the beatitude, "Blessed are the merciful: for they shall obtain mercy" (Matt. 5:7). From laboring in the fields of social reform to nurturing the beleaguered remnants of creation, the Third Order's endeavors manifest the scriptural axiom, "The earth is the Lord's, and the fulness thereof" (Ps. 24:1). Through generations of unfaltering devotion, their heroic works have woven an indelible tapestry of grace, binding the wounds of a fractured world and cultivating a sanctuary of peace and fraternity, forever adhering to the divine ordinance of stewardship and kinship.

Social Justice and Charity Work

The seeds of social justice and charitable work that the Third Order Regular Franciscans have sown over the centuries are numerous and deeply rooted in the teachings of St. Francis of Assisi. The vision of St. Francis, characterized by a profound commitment to poverty, humility, and service to the marginalized, set a robust foundation for the Order's endeavor in social justice and charity. The Franciscans tirelessly work to reflect the compassion of Christ, manifesting the words of Proverbs, "He that hath pity upon the poor lendeth unto the Lord" (Prov. 19:17).

From their beginnings, the Franciscans extended their hands to the poor and the downtrodden. They were among the first groups to advocate for the rights and well-being of the marginalized in the medieval era. Their approach wasn't solely motivated by compassion; it was a spiritual mission to see Christ in every suffering face and to serve Him by serving others. In a world that often neglects the destitute, the Franciscans' narrative offers a resounding counterpoint, echoing the directive of Jesus, "Inasmuch as ye have done it unto one of the least of these my brethren, ye have done it unto me" (Matt. 25:40).

Education sits at the heart of the Franciscans' social justice mission. The Order established myriad schools and universities, aiming to offer knowledge and skills to those who might otherwise be deprived. They viewed education not merely as an academic pursuit, but as a pathway to elevate human dignity and foster equality. By educating the minds and hearts of thousands, the Order promoted a just society where everyone could realize their God-given potential.

The Franciscans have also been pivotal in healthcare and the establishment of hospitals. They understood that physical and spiritual well-being are intertwined, and before modern medicine became a widespread field, they provided essential care. In times of plague, famine, and war, the Franciscans stood as beacons of mercy, continually present among the afflicted. The 'Hospital Brothers of St. Francis' were renowned for their dedication, embodying James' exhortation, "Pure religion and undefiled before God and the Father is this, To visit the fatherless and widows in their affliction" (James 1:27).

Their charitable work extended far beyond the boundaries of Europe. As the Franciscans journeyed to other continents, they carried the mandate of social justice with them. In the Americas, Africa, Asia, and Oceania, they far-reachingly impacted countless lives. From advocating against slavery to assisting in the aftermath of natural disasters, their purpose remained unchangeable: love in action, reflecting God's compassion.

Moreover, the Third Order's dedication to social justice is visible in their environmental stewardship. Following St. Francis, who is often regarded as the patron saint of ecology, they regard care for the Earth as a responsibility entrusted by the Creator. This holistic vision of justice extends to all of creation, aligning with the mandate given in Genesis to "dress it and to keep it" (Gen. 2:15). Current initiatives include sustainable farming, theological reflection on environmental ethics, and participating in global discussions on climate change.

The Third Order also confronts systemic injustices. They advocate for policy changes that align with the principles of social justice, lobbying for laws that promote human dignity and protect the vulnerable. This work often involves a challenging interplay with political powers, yet the Franciscans steadfastly pursue their mission, grounded in the hope that "righteousness exalteth a nation" (Prov. 14:34).

In addition, the Franciscans have initiated and sustained countless outreach programs. Shelters for the homeless, food pantries, legal aid for the disadvantaged, and support for refugees demonstrate their versatile approach to charity. They work not as mere philanthropists but as disciples following the teachings of Christ. Through these programs, they aim to transform society by fostering communities where solidarity and fraternity thrive.

The Franciscans' work in social justice and charity is not merely an externally directed mission. They also commit to introspection and reform within their communities. Self-imposed simplicity and communal sharing in their convents and fraternities reflect a microcosm of the justice they seek to cultivate in the wider world. Their ethos reveals a radical departure from materialism and self-centered living, aspiring to be as the Acts of the Apostles describes: "And all that believed were together, and had all things common; and sold their possessions and goods, and parted them to all men, as every man had need." (Acts 2:44-45).

Collaboration and community involvement are cornerstones of Franciscan efforts. They work alongside other religious orders, secular organizations, and government entities to amplify their impact. Partnerships with non-profits and grassroots initiatives allow them to extend their reach and resourcefulness. The Franciscans' approach is often pragmatic, realizing that effective justice and charity work requires an integrated network of support systems. Their cooperative spirit embodies Paul's vision of the Church as a body with many parts, where every part is vital and interconnected (1 Cor. 12:12-27).

Ultimately, the Franciscan contribution to social justice and charity is profoundly theological, grounded in the Incarnation. They see their actions as participation in Christ's redemptive mission, a continuation of His healing and teaching ministry. Their work is a living theology, a testament that God's kingdom is breaking into the world wherever love, justice, and peace are actualized. In every act of kindness, in every system they challenge, in every heart they touch, the Franciscans reveal the face of Christ and proclaim the Gospel anew, "For I was an hungred, and ye gave me meat: I was thirsty, and ye gave me drink: I was a stranger, and ye took me in" (Matt. 25:35).

It is essential to underscore that their efforts in social justice and charity are both responses and calls to deeper spirituality. As they care for the poorest of the poor, the Franciscans invite all faithful to examine their own lives, to act justly, to love mercy, and to walk humbly with God (Mic. 6:8). They epitomize what it means to live the Gospel, encouraging others to partake in this sacred mission, reinforcing the belief that "faith, if it hath not works, is dead" (James 2:17).

In the labyrinth of history, the social justice and charity work of the Third Order Regular Franciscans stands as a profound narrative of love, commitment, and transformative power. Their story is not confined to dusty records or hallowed halls; it breathes through the lives they've touched and continues as an enduring beacon of hope and divine mercy.

Environmental Stewardship

In the tapestry of the Third Order Regular Franciscans' contributions to the world, few threads shine as brightly as their commitment to environmental stewardship. It is a legacy deeply rooted in the teachings of St. Francis of Assisi, who is often regarded as the patron saint of ecology. His love for all of God's creations is not merely a poetic sentiment but a clarion call echoed down the annals of history by those who have taken up the Franciscan mantle.

St. Francis's famous "Canticle of the Sun" serves as an epigraph to the Franciscan ethos of environmental care. In this hymn, he celebrates Brother Sun, Sister Moon, and all elements of creation as integral parts of God's magnificent tapestry. The spirit of St. Francis speaks through these words, beckoning us to "Praise and bless my Lord, and give Him thanks, and serve Him with great humility" (Dan. 3:57). The Third Order Regular has faithfully answered this call, embedding ecological responsibility into their daily practices and wider mission.

From the medieval period to the modern age, the Franciscans have been pioneers in integrating respect for the environment within their way of life. Their monasteries and retreat centers often serve as sanctuaries of biodiversity, meticulously maintained to reflect the sanctity of nature. These grounds are more than mere gardens or agricultural plots; they are sacred groves where the divine is manifest in every leaf and stream.

In contemporary times, the Third Order Regular continues this tradition of environmental stewardship through a variety of initiatives. Organic farming is one prominent example, where Franciscans ensure that their agricultural practices harmonize with the rhythms of nature. By eschewing harmful pesticides and embracing sustainable techniques, they cultivate not only the soil but also the soul. They live out the words, "The earth is the Lord's, and the fulness thereof; the world, and they that dwell therein" (Ps. 24:1).

The Franciscans' commitment extends beyond their own communities to embrace broader environmental advocacy. They partner with secular organizations, local communities, and even governments to promote eco-friendly policies. Through education and grassroots activism, they seek to awaken a sense of ecological responsibility in people everywhere. As stewards of creation, they emphasize the moral imperative to protect the planet for future generations.

Moreover, the Third Order Regular emphasizes the spiritual dimensions of environmental care. They recognize that protecting the Earth is not merely an ethical or utilitarian endeavor but a spiritual vocation. This perspective is in resonance with the Biblical injunction to "dress it and to keep it" (Gen. 2:15), a mandate given to Adam that echoes through time to every inhabitant of the planet. The Franciscans teach that ecological sins—such as pollution, deforestation, and climate change—are offenses against God and His creation.

Liturgical practices within the Franciscan tradition also reflect this environmental consciousness. Services often include prayers of thanksgiving for nature's gifts and invocations for the protection of endangered ecosystems. These liturgies are not confined to the walls of churches but are conducted outdoors, in forests, fields, and by rivers, where the congregation can physically engage with creation. The mere act of worship in natural settings becomes an act of environmental solidarity, a fulfillment of the Psalmist's proclamation, "Let the heavens rejoice, and let the earth be glad; let the sea roar, and the fulness thereof" (Ps. 96:11).

Another crucial aspect of Franciscan environmental stewardship is their educational outreach. Schools and universities founded by the Franciscans incorporate environmental education into their curricula, emphasizing the interconnectedness of all creation. Students are taught not just the science of ecology but also its theological and ethical dimensions. They learn that caring for the environment is a way of participating in God's ongoing creation, a form of worship and reverence.

Community involvement is another hallmark of Franciscan environmental stewardship. The Third Order Regular organizes local eco-clubs and environmental groups to engage communities in sustainable practices. These groups conduct clean-up drives, tree plantation campaigns, and workshops on sustainable living, embodying the call to "serve one another" (Gal. 5:13) through concrete action.

Importantly, the Franciscans do not view their environmental efforts as separate from their broader mission of social justice. They understand that environmental degradation often disproportionately affects the poor and marginalized, exacerbating social inequalities. Thus, their environmental stewardship goes hand-in-hand with their work for social justice and charity, reflecting the holistic vision of St. Francis.

In striving for a world that reflects divine love and justice, the Third Order Regular Franciscans embody the Apostle Paul's exhortation to be "stewards of the mysteries of God" (1 Cor. 4:1). Their environmental efforts are not merely practical necessities but profound acts of faith, expressions of a spirituality that sees the hand of God in every aspect of creation.

Through their commitment to environmental stewardship, the Franciscans teach us that the care of our world is a sacred duty, an expression of our love for the Creator. They remind us, as St.

Francis himself did, to see the face of God in all living things and to treat every aspect of creation with reverence and respect. Thus, in emulating the Franciscan way, we not only honor the Earth but also draw closer to the divine.

Chapter 5: Key Figures in Third Order History

In the annals of the Third Order Regular, God has raised illustrious pillars whose fervor and sanctity illuminated paths for the faithful: many have trod but few have shone as brightly as St. Elizabeth of Hungary and Blessed Angela of Foligno. St. Elizabeth, a princess turned servant of the poor, embodied the teaching of Matthew 25:35—"For I was an hungred, and ye gave me meat: I was thirsty, and ye gave me drink: I was a stranger, and ye took me in"—through her boundless charity and unwavering humility, becoming a living testament to the Franciscan charism. Meanwhile, Blessed Angela, once ensnared by worldly attachments, experienced a profound conversion that mirrored the prodigal son's return, leading her to extraordinary mystical depths and an unparalleled articulation of divine love and suffering. These holy figures, transcending the ages, continue to inspire and guide the Order in its mission to live out the Gospel with zeal and compassion, exemplifying the words of Proverbs 31:20—"She stretcheth out her hand to the poor; yea, she reacheth forth her hands to the needy"—in every action and prayer.

St. Elizabeth of Hungary

Amidst the illuminations of the 13th century, the world bore witness to the life of Saint Elizabeth of Hungary, a figure whose devotion to Franciscan ideals continues to resonate through the annals of history. Born in the year 1207, as a princess in the Kingdom of Hungary, Elizabeth's life seemed predestined for royal splendor. Yet, the Lord chose her for a path far removed from the luxuries of the court. Her heart was firmly bent towards the downtrodden, embodying the virtues of poverty and charity that are the cornerstone of Franciscan spirituality. "Blessed are the poor in spirit: for theirs is the kingdom of heaven" (Matt. 5:3). From her earliest days, Elizabeth displayed profound piety, and thus began the unfolding of a sanctified life deeply entwined with the Third Order of Saint Francis.

At the tender age of four, Elizabeth was betrothed to Louis IV of Thuringia, a political maneuver common in medieval Europe. The union was one not merely of convenience but of divine orchestration, for both Louis and Elizabeth shared an unwavering commitment to their faith. Their marriage, consecrated in 1221, transformed the Wartburg Castle into a citadel of charity. They set an example as learned Scripture scholars, looking to Christ's model of service and sacrifice. Elizabeth would often hide bread in her cloak to feed the poor, and legend recounts that when confronted by her husband, the bread miraculously turned into roses, a sign of divine approval. "He that hath pity upon the poor lendeth unto the Lord" (Prov. 19:17).

Elizabeth's commitment to Franciscan principles became ever more rigorous following Louis's untimely death during the Crusades in 1227. At twenty years old and stricken with grief, Elizabeth took a vow of celibacy and relinquished her claim to worldly possessions, embracing the path of a penitent. She donned the grey habit of the Third Order, renouncing royalty for a life of humility and service. "Whosoever will come after me, let him deny himself, and take up his cross, and follow me" (Mark 8:34). This period was marked by immense personal transformation, encapsulating the Franciscan ideals of living in solidarity with the marginalized.

In Marburg, Elizabeth devoted herself to the sick and destitute, founding a hospital and personally tending to the afflicted. Her work was not mere philanthropy but an act of love, mirroring Christ's compassion for the least among us. The hospital became a haven where the spiritual and corporal works of mercy converged, offering not only medical care but also solace and hope. Her life was a vivid sermon, an embodiment of the beatitudes, especially "Blessed are the merciful: for they shall obtain mercy" (Matt. 5:7). Elizabeth's sanctity was manifested through her tireless efforts to alleviate suffering, reflecting a heart fully surrendered to God.

The last years of her brief life were marked by increasing austerity. Elizabeth's ascetic practices and fervent piety did not go unnoticed. Her spiritual director, Conrad of Marburg, imposed rigorous disciplines that Elizabeth accepted with Christ-like humility. Despite this, hers was not a spirit broken, but one fortified by divine grace. Her relentless dedication to the Franciscan way of life continued unimpeded until her death at the age of twenty-four in 1231. The impact of her life was such that she was canonized by Pope Gregory IX only four years later, in 1235. "For they shall be called children of God" (Matt. 5:9).

Elizabeth's legacy is not merely confined to hagiographies but extends through the spiritual edifice she helped to build. Her life serves as a paradigm of the Franciscan mission to adore Christ in simplicity, poverty, and charity. Her deep union with the sufferings of Christ and her boundless love for the poor serve as both inspiration and challenge to all who tread the Franciscan path. Her relics and the hospital she founded became pilgrimage sites, symbolizing a perennial source of grace and intercession. "For where your treasure is, there will your heart be also" (Matt. 6:21).

In an era marked by significant socio-political transformations, Elizabeth's life offers enduring lessons. Her embrace of the Third Order Regular was not an escape from her noble duties but a transcendence of them. She exemplified the possibility of holiness in the secular realm, an ardent reminder that every act of genuine love towards one's neighbor is a participation in Christ's redemptive work. In her, we see a profound synthesis of contemplation and action, a serene yet zealous proclamation of the Gospel through deeds.

Saint Elizabeth of Hungary stands as a luminous figure in the history of the Third Order. Her narrative weaves through the tapestry of Franciscan heritage, echoing the divine call to love without bounds, serve without recognition, and live without fear. Through her life and works, she illuminates the quintessential Franciscan journey, a pilgrimage of the soul towards the heart of God, where love is the measure of all things and service is the language of faith. Indeed, her sanctified path beckons us to think deeply and act justly, continuing her mission in a world ever in need of divine compassion.

Blessed Angela of Foligno

In the illustrious history of the Third Order Regular Franciscans, few figures stand out as prominently as Blessed Angela of Foligno. Her life, marked by profound spiritual experiences and radical conversion, offers a compelling testament to the transformative power of faith. Born into a well-off family in Foligno, Italy, around 1248, Angela initially led a life far removed from piety. However, the course of her life changed dramatically following a series of personal tragedies and mystical visions. These experiences propelled her to embrace a life of penance, poverty, and deep union with God.

Angela's spiritual journey began in earnest following the deaths of her mother, husband, and children within a short span of time. Finding herself bereft of familial attachments, she sought solace and meaning through the teachings of St. Francis of Assisi. Her early years of spiritual searching were fraught with inner turmoil and a profound sense of unworthiness. It was during this period of intense introspection and prayer that she experienced a series of mystical visions that would define her spiritual trajectory.

Embracing the Franciscan way of life, Angela adopted an austere lifestyle, characterized by self-denial and charitable works. She became known for her extreme penances and acts of charity, distributing her wealth to the poor and dedicating herself to the care of the sick and marginalized. Her spirituality was deeply rooted in the Franciscan tradition, emphasizing humility, simplicity, and a profound love for the Crucified Christ. Angela's writings, most notably her spiritual autobiography, reveal a soul consumed by divine love and longing for union with God.

Angela's mystical experiences are meticulously documented in her "Memorial," a spiritual autobiography dictated to her confessor, Brother Arnold. This text offers a vivid account of her interior life and mystical encounters. Notably, her visions were often Christocentric, focusing on the Passion of Christ and the mysteries of the Church. Her descriptions, rich in biblical allusions and theological depth, provide a profound insight into her intimate communion with the Divine.

In one of her most significant visions, Angela recounts an encounter with Christ in which she feels an encompassing sense of divine love and mercy. This experience culminated in what she described as a mystical union, wherein she felt wholly united with God. The "Memorial" is replete with such instances, showcasing her deepening journey toward spiritual perfection and union with the Divine. "For where your treasure is, there will your heart be also" (Matt. 6:21).

Moreover, Angela's spiritual teachings continue to resonate within the Franciscan tradition. Her emphasis on the centrality of Christ's Passion as a path to spiritual enlightenment has influenced countless followers. The sacrificial love depicted in her visions echoes the scriptural call to take up the cross and follow Christ, as found in the Gospels. "And he that taketh not his cross, and followeth after me, is not worthy of me" (Matt. 10:38).

Angela's life and works were not just limited to personal piety; she also had a significant impact on her contemporaries. Her charismatic personality and profound spiritual insights drew many to seek her guidance. She became a revered spiritual mother to numerous disciples, guiding them toward a deeper relationship with God. Her communal gatherings, known as the "School of Divine Love," provided spiritual formation and encouragement to her followers.

Her sanctity was recognized by the Church many centuries after her death. Angela of Foligno was beatified by Pope Innocent XII in 1693, a testament to her enduring influence and the Church's recognition of her mystical experiences and spiritual teachings. Her beatification serves as a reminder of the universality of the call to holiness, irrespective of one's initial life circumstances.

The life of Blessed Angela of Foligno is a beacon of hope for those who find themselves in the depths of despair, illustrating that it is never too late for conversion. Her story resonates with the biblical parable of the prodigal son, a reminder of God's boundless mercy and the transformative power of repentance. "I say unto you, that likewise joy shall be in heaven over one sinner that repenteth, more than over ninety and nine just persons, which need no repentance" (Luke 15:7).

Angela's legacy continues to inspire not just the Franciscans but the entire Christian community. Her life demonstrates the profound joy and peace that comes from living a life wholly surrendered to God. Her mystical experiences offer a unique insight into the soul's journey toward divine union, encouraging the faithful to seek a deeper relationship with Christ.

In reflecting on Angela's life, one is reminded of the timeless truth of the Gospel—that in losing oneself, one truly finds oneself. Angela's journey from worldly pursuits to spiritual enlightenment exemplifies the transformative potential of divine grace. It offers a poignant reminder of Jesus' words: "For whosoever will save his life shall lose it: and whosoever will lose his life for my sake shall find it" (Matt. 16:25).

Today, the writings and teachings of Blessed Angela of Foligno continue to be a source of spiritual richness within the Third Order Regular Franciscans. Her life story, marked by intense suffering, personal tragedy, and eventual union with God, remains an enduring testament to the transformative power of faith. As scholars and theologians continue to study her life and works, the depth of her spiritual insights and the universality of her message only grow more apparent.

Angela stands as a luminous example of the resilience of the human spirit and the boundless mercy of God. Her life story, chronicled meticulously in her "Memorial," offers invaluable wisdom and guidance for those seeking a deeper relationship with God. Her beatification underscores the Church's recognition of her unique contributions to Christian spirituality and the Franciscan tradition.

In conclusion, Blessed Angela of Foligno exemplifies the core values of the Franciscan tradition: humility, compassion, and a profound love for Christ. Her life serves as a powerful exemplar of the transformative power of divine grace, offering hope and inspiration to all who seek to follow the path of holiness. Her legacy, enshrined in her writings and the lives of her followers, continues to illuminate the path to spiritual fulfillment and union with God.

Chapter 6: Franciscan University of Steubenville

The Franciscan University of Steubenville stands as a beacon of both academic rigor and spiritual fervor, a testament to the enduring legacy of the Third Order Regular. Established in 1946 under the watchful gaze of the Most Reverend Bishop John King Mussio, the institution quickly burgeoned into a cornerstone of Catholic education, fostering intellectual and spiritual growth through an unwavering commitment to the teachings of Christ and St. Francis. "And Jesus increased in wisdom and stature, and in favour with God and man" (Luke 2:52). This sacred mission manifests in its rigorous academic programs and vibrant campus ministry, each harmonizing to nurture scholars who are as devout as they are learned. The university's ethos, deeply rooted in the Franciscan tradition, champions an education that is as transformative as it is informative, knitting together faith and reason in a tapestry that has become the very fabric of its community. Through its halls echo the prayers and aspirations of countless students and faculty, each striving to embody the virtues of humility, service, and love for all creation. In this revered place of learning, the spirit of St. Francis lives on, illuminating paths not just to careers, but to vocations of the highest order.

Founding and Mission

The establishment of the Franciscan University of Steubenville is a testament to the enduring vision that resonates through the halls of Franciscan spirituality: a synthesis of faith, reason, and the pursuit of knowledge. Its inception stemmed from the recognition that education was not merely an acquisition of facts but an arena to mold minds and hearts in accordance with divine wisdom. The university's founders, deeply imbued with Franciscan ideals, aimed to craft an institution where academic excellence walks hand in hand with spiritual growth.

The roots of this noble endeavor can be traced back to the mid-20th century, a time when the world wrestled with the aftermath of global conflict and societal upheaval. It was during this turbulent period that Steubenville, Ohio, saw the birth of what would become a beacon of Catholic higher education. The mission was clear: to provide a holistic formation that integrates the intellectual, moral, and spiritual dimensions of each student, preparing them for lives of faithful service and leadership.

At the heart of this mission lies a profound commitment to the teachings of Christ, evoking the words of Jesus as recorded in the Gospel of John: "And ye shall know the truth, and the truth shall make you free" (John 8:32). This scriptural mandate underscores the university's dedication to exploring and embodying Truth, which is Christ Himself. Thus, academic pursuits are not ends in themselves but means to encounter and serve the Divine.

The foundational spirit of the Franciscan University of Steubenville is encapsulated in the charism of St. Francis of Assisi, whose revolutionary approach to living the Gospel continues to inspire. Francis's radical embrace of poverty, humility, and peace serves as a guiding star, exhorting the university community to seek a life that mirrors Christ's own. The Franciscan emphasis on simplicity and joy infuses the atmosphere, inviting students and faculty alike to find divine beauty in the ordinary and the everyday.

A key element in realizing this vision is the integration of faith and reason, two wings by which the soul rises to contemplation of the truth. Inspired by the Scholastic tradition, the university emphasizes rigorous intellectual inquiry balanced with unwavering fidelity to Church teachings. This dynamic interplay fosters an environment where theological insights enliven academic disciplines, and scholarly endeavors reinforce spiritual convictions.

Another cornerstone of the university's mission is the sanctification of the whole person. This echoes the apostle Paul's exhortation: "And the very God of peace sanctify you wholly;

and I pray God your whole spirit and soul and body be preserved blameless unto the coming of our Lord Jesus Christ" (1 Thess. 5:23). Recognizing the intrinsic unity of body, mind, and spirit, the university offers numerous opportunities for spiritual enrichment, including daily Mass, Eucharistic adoration, retreats, and spiritual direction. These avenues of grace aim to form individuals who are not only intellectually competent but spiritually vibrant and morally steadfast.

Central to the Franciscan University's identity is its commitment to evangelization. This mission resonates with the Great Commission entrusted to the apostles: "Go ye therefore, and teach all nations" (Matt. 28:19). This evangelical thrust manifests in various ways: academic programs designed to equip students for missionary work, dynamic campus ministries, and extensive outreach efforts both locally and globally. The aim is to cultivate evangelizers who are intellectually robust, spiritually passionate, and culturally astute.

Moreover, the Franciscan University of Steubenville remains a testament to prophetic courage, challenging contemporary cultural mores with the timeless truths of the Gospel. The university stands as a counter-cultural witness, proclaiming the sanctity of life, the dignity of marriage, and the beauty of human sexuality in accord with Church teaching. This resolute stance often draws opposition, yet it also engenders a deep respect and admiration from those who recognize the integrity and consistency of the university's mission.

The mission of the Franciscan University extends beyond its immediate community. It aspires to be a leaven in the world, transforming societies through the Gospel's power. Graduates are encouraged to carry the Franciscan ethos into their respective vocations, embodying St. Francis's prayer: "Lord, make me an instrument of thy peace." In fields as diverse as business, healthcare, education, and the arts, alumni are challenged to be channels of God's peace and love, sowing seeds of hope in a fractured world.

Fundamentally, the Franciscan University's mission is best understood as a living tradition, an ongoing narrative that interweaves the past with the present while eagerly anticipating the future. Each academic institution, each spiritual program, and each act of charity participates in this grand tapestry, continually weaving new threads of hope and renewal. The founders' visionary zeal thus finds its continuity in every classroom discussion, every heartfelt prayer, and every act of service performed by the university community.

Indeed, the Franciscan University of Steubenville is a testament to the enduring power of a vision animated by faith. It embodies a prophetic witness, bearing the light of Christ to the ends of the earth, anchored in the rich spirituality of the Franciscan tradition. As the university continues to grow and evolve, it remains unwavering in its commitment to form individuals who, in the words of St. Paul, can confidently affirm, "I am made all things to all men, that I might by all means save some" (1 Cor. 9:22). The Franciscan University's founding and mission, therefore, stand as a beacon, illuminating the path to wholeness and sanctity in an ever-changing world.

Academic and Spiritual Contributions

The Franciscan University of Steubenville, rooted in the charism of St. Francis of Assisi, seamlessly blends academic rigor with deep spiritual formation. This unique institution stands as a beacon of light in a world thirsting for both knowledge and spiritual nourishment. The University's commitment to educating the whole person—mind, body, and spirit—echoes through its curriculums, campus life, and community engagements.

Founded in 1946, Franciscan University has always aimed to offer more than mere academic instruction. From its inception, the mission was clear: to cultivate both intellectual and spiritual excellence. The ethos of the University is captured in its motto, "Sanctitas et Scientia"—"Holiness and Knowledge". This harmonization of piety and scholarly pursuit is evident in every facet of the University.

The academic offerings at Franciscan University are diverse and comprehensive, ranging from Theology and Philosophy to the Natural Sciences and Business Administration. These programs are meticulously designed to align with the University's mission of forming students who are intellectually competent and spiritually grounded. Here, education is seen as a vocation, a calling to explore the mysteries of creation with reverence and awe.

Integral to the University's academic landscape is its commitment to the liberal arts tradition. This tradition fosters critical thinking, eloquence in speech and writing, and a broadened horizon. The study of literature, history, and the arts is not merely for intellectual stimulation but is viewed as a pathway to better understand human nature and, ultimately, God. For "the heavens declare the glory of God; and the firmament sheweth his handywork" (Psalm 19:1).

Yet, the soul of Franciscan University goes beyond intellectual pursuits; it profoundly interweaves spiritual formation into the student experience. Daily Mass, perpetual adoration, and the opportunity for sacramental confession are staples of campus life. These practices ground the academic endeavors in a life of prayer and reflection, ensuring that students not only gain knowledge but also wisdom.

Moreover, the University places a high premium on community life, which is seen as an essential component of the Franciscan educational experience. Students are encouraged to engage in community service and outreach programs. These programs not only benefit the wider community but also instill in students a sense of responsibility and compassion. As it is written, "Bear ye one another's burdens, and so fulfill the law of Christ" (Galatians 6:2).

A distinctive feature of the University's spiritual contribution is its dedication to evangelization. Through various ministries, students are trained and inspired to share the Good News both locally and globally. Programs like the Household System, a unique form of voluntary fraternity and sorority life, provide a support network that fosters both spiritual growth and accountability. In these households, students pray together, study scripture, and support one another in their faith journeys.

Faculty members at Franciscan University play a crucial role in this dual mission of academic and spiritual excellence. Professors are not merely teachers but mentors and role models in living a Christ-centered life. They challenge students to integrate faith with reason and to seek truth in all disciplines. Through their scholarship and witness, they embody the University's mission, encouraging students to see their studies as part of their larger vocation to serve God and humanity.

One cannot overlook the University's vibrant campus ministry, which offers an array of spiritual programs. Retreats, missions, and spiritual direction are readily available, nurturing the spiritual lives of students, faculty, and staff. With an emphasis on

Eucharistic worship and Marian devotion, these programs cultivate a deep and abiding love for Christ and His Church.

In addition to the spiritual life, the University's arts program also contributes to the holistic education emphasized in Franciscan tradition. Theater, music, and visual arts are all celebrated as mediums through which the Creator's beauty is manifested. Students are encouraged to develop their artistic talents, which in turn serve as expressions of divine creativity and instruments for evangelization.

The University's Franciscan facilities and architecture themselves are testimonies to the integration of the spiritual and the academic. The Portiuncula Chapel, a replica of the chapel rebuilt by St. Francis, offers a place of solitude and prayer. Surrounding the chapel, various statues and art pieces serve as visual reminders of the University's spiritual heritage, creating an environment that inspires contemplation and study.

The global reach of Franciscan University also testifies to its significant contributions. Through study abroad programs, particularly in Austria, students gain a broader perspective of the Catholic intellectual tradition and deepen their spiritual lives in diverse cultural contexts. These experiences are formative, grounding students in a universal faith that transcends geographical boundaries.

To further these ends, the University fosters relationships with other Catholic institutions and orders across the globe, engaging in dialogues that enrich both its academic and spiritual life. Such collaborative endeavors ensure that the University remains at the forefront of both theological inquiry and pastoral practice.

In recent years, the University has also embraced digital platforms to extend its evangelistic and educational efforts. Online degree programs, virtual conferences, and digital resources make Franciscan's revered educational experience accessible to a worldwide audience. This approach not only meets contemporary needs but also brings the gospel's transformative power to people in every corner of the world.

Moreover, the emphasis on social justice and ethical leadership prepares students to confront and address the moral dilemmas of our times. Whether through service-learning projects, internships, or advocacy, students are equipped to be agents of change who uphold the principles of peace and justice championed by St. Francis.

Indeed, Franciscan University of Steubenville is not just an academic institution; it is a community of believers committed to living out the gospel. Its academic programs and spiritual practices are harmoniously aligned to form individuals who are not only competent in their disciplines but also ardent in their faith. They emerge not just as graduates but as disciples ready to serve the Church and the world.

In conclusion, the contributions of Franciscan University of Steubenville are manifold. Its blend of academic excellence and spiritual formation shapes leaders who are equipped to confront the challenges of the modern world with faith and reason. This legacy of holistic education invites all to a deeper appreciation of truth, beauty, and goodness, grounded in the rich tradition of St. Francis and the broader Catholic Church. As it is written: "And the grace of our Lord was exceeding abundant with faith and love which is in Christ Jesus" (1 Timothy 1:14).

Chapter 7: Third Order Saints and Their Legacy

The legacy of Third Order saints shines with celestial clarity across centuries, manifesting God's grace and love in the mortal realm. St. Louis IX of France, renowned for his piety and just rule, embodies the fusion of sanctity and sovereignty, leading his kingdom as a steward of divine will. St. Roch, another luminary, walked among the afflicted, healing with the mere touch of his hand, a living testament to Matthew's exhortation: "Heal the sick, cleanse the lepers, raise the dead, cast out devils: freely ye have received, freely give" (Matt. 10:8). These saints, among countless others, inscribed their fervent devotion on the hearts of the faithful, infusing the world with the Franciscan charism of humility, charity, and unwavering fidelity to Christ's teachings. Their lives, interwoven with divine and human threads, continue to inspire and guide the Franciscans of today, a heritage reflecting the eternal light of God's kingdom.

St. Louis IX of France

In the annals of the Franciscan Third Order, few figures are as luminous as St. Louis IX of France. As the only French king to be canonized, his legacy not only illuminates the path of sanctity but also embodies the synthesis of royal duty and divine calling. Born in 1214, he ascended to the throne at a tender age, and throughout his reign, he demonstrated an unparalleled commitment to justice, charity, and the Christian faith.

King Louis IX was not just a monarch; he was a reflection of the Franciscan ethos in action. Deeply inspired by St. Francis of Assisi, Louis sought to infuse his reign with the same principles of humility, poverty, and piety that had characterized the Poverello of Assisi. His association with the Third Order Franciscans offered him a roadmap for governing with a heart imbued with compassion. He was renowned for washing the feet of lepers, feeding the poor, and establishing hospitals and charitable institutions. In many ways, he lived out the biblical exhortation, "Whatsoever ye do to the least of my brethren, ye have done it unto me" (Matt. 25:40).

St. Louis's dedication to justice was legendary. He created ordinances to ensure fair treatment for all his subjects, regardless of their status or wealth. He held court under the Oak of Vincennes, personally listening to the grievances of his people. This personal touch in governance reflected the Franciscan spirit of fraternity and equality. His justice, steeped in Christian morality, was both a reflection and a projection of the divine justice of God.

Louis IX's commitment to the Crusades, though controversial in contemporary perspectives, was driven by a profound sense of religious duty. He viewed the Holy Land as a sacred heritage that required protection and reclamation. His actions were guided by a belief in the salvific enterprise of the Crusades, aiming to safeguard and sanctify the sites central to Christian faith. His two Crusade expeditions, though fraught with challenges and ultimate failure, represented his indomitable spirit and unwavering faith.

Beyond his royal and military endeavors, Louis IX was a devoted family man and a spiritual pillar to his court and nation. He fostered an environment of devotion and learning within his family, ensuring his children were brought up with deep religious convictions. His patronage of books and scholarly works significantly contributed to the intellectual and theological wealth of his time. His household became a microcosm of a Christian community, exemplifying the Franciscan familial spirit.

St. Louis IX's canonization in 1297, twenty-seven years after his death, was a testament to his enduring sanctity and influence. The Church recognized in him a paragon of Christian kingship, a ruler whose earthy crown and heavenly aspiration were seamlessly intertwined. His feast day, celebrated on August 25, serves as a perennial reminder of the virtues he embodied and the legacy he left.

The influence of St. Louis IX on the Third Order Franciscans is immeasurable. His life stands as a guiding star for those within the Order, demonstrating that one can harmonize temporal power with spiritual depth. His governance was not merely about wielding power but about serving his people with the humility of Christ. This legacy of service before self remains a cornerstone of Franciscan spirituality.

In an era where the lines between the sacred and secular were often blurred, St. Louis IX showcased how they could be intertwined to create a tapestry of divine grace and human effort. He did not retreat from the world to seek God; instead, he sought God's presence in the world, especially among the marginalized and forgotten. This profound integration of faith into every aspect of his rule and life is a legacy that continues to resonate within the Third Order Franciscans.

Moreover, Louis's dedication to the Church and its teachings extended beyond mere piety; it was an active engagement in fostering religious and educational institutions. The foundations he laid for various monastic communities and schools fostered a culture of learning and devotion that would inspire generations to come. His contributions helped to fortify the intellectual and spiritual framework of his kingdom, solidifying the symbiotic relationship between state and church.

The sanctity of St. Louis IX serves as a beacon for what it means to live out the Franciscan charism in the world. It's a call to witness, to evangelize not just through words but through actions imbued with love and justice. Louis IX's life invites the members of the Third Order and indeed all Christians to a deeper reflection on how one can embody the Gospel values in their respective vocations, whether secular or sacred.

In summation, the saga of St. Louis IX of France is an epic of divine purpose intersecting with royal obligation. Through his life and deeds, one can see the traces of God weaving through the fabric of history, guiding and shaping a king who would become a saint. His legacy is far-reaching, touching lives across centuries and continents through the continued mission and dedication of the Third Order Franciscans. As they pursue their vocation, the memory of St. Louis IX serves as a perpetual source of inspiration and a testament to the transformative power of a life lived in complete fidelity to God's will.

St. Roch

Among the illustrious saints who have graced the annals of Franciscan history, St. Roch occupies a unique and venerable place. Born in the late 13th century in Montpellier, France, St. Roch's life is a tapestry woven with threads of humility, charity, and miraculous intercession. His journey exemplifies the Franciscan virtues of poverty, simplicity, and profound compassion for the suffering, thereby elevating him as a luminary within the Third Order's celestial firmament.

St. Roch was born into a noble family, yet his early inclination towards piety and asceticism set him apart from the trappings of wealth and status. Orphaned in his youth, he distributed his inheritance to the poor and joined the Third Order of St. Francis. Thus commenced his pilgrimage across Europe, a journey not merely of physical distance but of spiritual magnitude. As he traveled, his heart was moved by the plight of the sick, particularly those ravaged by the plague—a scourge that decimated communities and instilled fear in the hearts of men.

According to the hallowed traditions, St. Roch's ministry began in the Italian city of Aquapendente, where he encountered plague-stricken souls abandoned by all but divine providence. In this crucible of suffering, St. Roch's faith was a balm as he tended to the afflicted, training his gaze not on the grotesque lesions that marked their bodies but on the divine spark that animated their beings. His mere presence was said to invoke miraculous healings, drawing an ever-growing circle of devotees and beneficiaries of his sanctity.

The life of St. Roch is punctuated by his own battle with the plague, which serves as a testament to his solidarity with those he served. Stricken while in Piacenza, he retreated to a forest to shield others from contagion. There, weakened and alone, he was sustained by a faithful dog who, by divine inspiration, brought him bread and licked his wounds, facilitating his recovery. This touching episode underscores the interconnectedness of all God's creatures and reminds us that divine assistance often comes from the most unexpected quarters.

In the depths of his isolation and suffering, St. Roch exemplified Christ's own passion and endurance. Isaiah's prophecy resonates in his life: "Surely he hath borne our griefs, and carried our sorrows" (Isaiah 53:4). Such profound empathy with human tribulation elevated St. Roch from mere healer to an icon of redemptive suffering.

Upon his recovery, St. Roch resumed his mission of mercy, his renown preceding him. Cities like Rome and Cesena marked their gratitude with statues and churches, forever enshrining his legacy in stone as well as spirit. Yet his earthly journey concluded under clouds of misunderstanding and martyrdom; upon returning to Montpellier, he was imprisoned as a spy as he was unrecognized due to his self-imposed anonymity. He accepted this unjust suffering with the grace and dignity that had defined his life, embracing imprisonment as another facet of his divine mission.

The culmination of St. Roch's life came with his death within the confines of his cell. It was only after his passing that his true identity was revealed, prompting a cascade of miracles which affirmed his sainthood. As the gospel recounts, "For there is nothing covered, that shall not be revealed; neither hid, that shall not be known" (Luke 12:2). Posthumously, his relics became powerful sources of intercession, prompting the construction of basilicas in his honor and ensuring his veneration among the faithful for centuries to come.

St. Roch's legacy extends beyond geographical and temporal confines, inspiring devotions and communities dedicated to his example. His life and deeds are commemorated annually on August 16, with liturgical celebrations that reflect upon his virtues and invoke his protection against pestilence. In the Franciscan tradition, his story offers a myriad of lessons: a relentless quest for spiritual purity, an unyielding commitment to serve the destitute, and a profound trust in God's providence.

More than a historical figure, St. Roch stands as a paragon of Franciscan spirituality for contemporary believers. His imprint is especially poignant in today's contexts of global health crises and social upheaval. The ethos of St. Roch—one of endless charity and unwavering faith—serves as a beacon for Third Order Franciscans and laypersons alike, calling them to embody Christ's love in a fractured world.

The life and legacy of St. Roch remind us of the eternal truth encapsulated in the Beatitudes: "Blessed are the merciful: for they shall obtain mercy" (Matt. 5:7). His mercy, extended to the least of these in their hour of agony, reverberates through the centuries, inviting all who hear his story to walk the path he trod, marked by sacrifice, compassion, and divine grace.

As we reflect on his life, we are called to emulate his virtues, seek his intercession, and trust in the divine care that sustained him. In doing so, we not only honor St. Roch but also draw closer to the heart of the Franciscan mission: to live in selfless love for God and neighbor, transcending the temporal to touch the eternal.

Chapter 8: Theology and Writings

Within the perennial verdure of the Third Order Regular Franciscans lies a robust theological tapestry, richly woven with the threads of divine inspiration and scholarly diligence. Their theological contributions resound with echoes of the early Church Fathers, harmonizing profound spirituality with intellectual rigour. Embedded in this fabric are texts that illuminate facets of divine truth, akin to luminous stars in the firmament of Christian thought, guiding the faithful through the complexities of doctrinal understanding. Eminent authors such as St. Bonaventure and John Duns Scotus have imparted luminary insights that shape our grasp of creation, redemption, and sanctification. Their works resound the call to "study to shew thyself approved unto God" (2 Tim. 2:15), compelling Franciscans to unite erudition with fervent devotion. This sacred synthesis of contemplation and action, bound by a commitment to humility and charity, manifests in writings that not only edify but transform. Hence, the annals of the Third Order's theology and writings stand as a testament to their enduring mission, encapsulating the essence of their spiritual journey and theological depth.

Major Theological Contributions

The Third Order Regular of St. Francis, often heralded for embodying a spirituality that is both transcendent and rooted in everyday life, has made enduring theological contributions to the Church. With origins tracing back to the radical vision of St. Francis of Assisi, the Third Order has consistently distilled complex theological principles into accessible practices and teachings. Their theological legacy, imbued with the essence of Gospel living, reflects a profound commitment to the core tenets of Christian faith.

From its inception, the Third Order Regular encapsulated St. Francis's emphasis on the Incarnation. The mystery of God becoming flesh, as elucidated in John 1:14, "And the Word was made flesh, and dwelt among us" (John 1:14), serves as the cornerstone of their theological reflections. Franciscans viewed the Incarnation not just as a historical event but as an ongoing reality that shapes and informs their ministry. In this light, their theology embraces a holistic view of creation, seeing the presence of the divine in all of life.

Another seminal contribution of the Third Order is their theology of poverty and humility. Inspired by Christ's own poverty, their understanding of voluntary poverty transcends mere material deprivation. It is seen as an act of profound spiritual liberation and solidarity with the marginalized. This theological vision is grounded in the Sermon on the Mount, particularly the Beatitudes, where Jesus declares, "Blessed are the poor in spirit: for theirs is the kingdom of heaven" (Matt. 5:3). Through such teachings, the Third Order has offered a compelling counter-narrative to the consumerism and materialism prevalent in society.

Furthermore, the Franciscans' theology of creation is integral to their identity. They espouse a sacramental view of nature, seeing every element of creation as a reflection of God's beauty and goodness. This theological stance is rooted in the scriptural affirmation of creation's inherent goodness, as found in Genesis 1:31, "And God saw every thing that he had made, and, behold, it was very good" (Gen. 1:31). By cultivating a deep reverence for nature, the Third Order has significantly contributed to contemporary ecological theology and environmental ethics.

In their theological treatises and writings, the Third Order frequently emphasizes the kenosis, or self-emptying, of Christ as described in Philippians 2:7, "But made himself of no reputation, and took upon him the form of a servant, and was made in the likeness of men" (Phil. 2:7). This theme resonates deeply in their spiritual practices and communal living, where members are encouraged to embrace humility, simplicity, and service. The concept of kenosis also informs their approach to leadership, fostering a model that is collaborative and grounded in servant leadership.

The Third Order's theological reflections on peace and reconciliation are equally noteworthy. Influenced by St. Francis's own peace-making efforts, their theology underscores the transformative power of forgiveness and reconciliation. They draw inspiration from Christ's commandment in Matthew 5:9, "Blessed are the peacemakers: for they shall be called the children of God" (Matt. 5:9). This commitment to peace is not just theoretical but is lived out through various ministries and social justice initiatives, bridging divides and fostering unity.

Additionally, the Third Order's emphasis on communal life offers a rich theological legacy. They have developed a theology of fraternity, where community life is seen as a microcosm of the larger Body of Christ. This perspective is deeply scriptural, reflecting the early Christian communities described in Acts 2:44-47, "And all that believed were together, and had all things common; And sold their possessions and goods, and parted them to all men, as every man had need" (Acts 2:44-45). Through their communal practices, members of the Third Order witness to the possibility of living out the Gospel values in a collective context.

Moreover, their theological contributions include a robust understanding of the Eucharist. For the Franciscans, the Eucharist is not merely a sacrament to be celebrated but a profound mystery to be lived. This theology is anchored in Jesus' words at the Last Supper, "This is my body which is given for you: this do in remembrance of me" (Luke 22:19). The emphasis on the Eucharist fosters a spirituality of presence, hospitality, and sacrificial love, impacting both their liturgical life and everyday interactions.

The Third Order has also contributed significantly to Mariology, the theological study of Mary. They venerate Mary as the Mother of God and the perfect disciple, echoing the angelic greeting, "Hail, thou that art highly favoured, the Lord is with thee: blessed art thou among women" (Luke 1:28). Their devotion to Mary influences their understanding of discipleship, emphasizing obedience, purity, and openness to God's will. This Marian devotion is seamlessly integrated into their theology, enriching their spiritual practices and doctrinal teachings.

In addition to these themes, Third Order theologians have consistently worked on developing theological anthropology, the study of humanity in the light of divine revelation. By focusing on the dignity and worth of every individual, they echo the biblical affirmation that humans are made in the image and likeness of God (Gen. 1:27). This theological perspective has profound ethical implications, driving the Order's commitment to human rights, social justice, and advocacy for the oppressed.

Significantly, their contributions extend to eschatology, the theology of the last things. The Third Order teaches a hopeful eschatology, filled with the expectation of the final fulfillment of God's kingdom. This is rooted in Christ's promise in John 14:2-3, "In my Father's house are many mansions: if it were not so, I would have told you. I go to prepare a place for you. And if I go and prepare a place for you, I will come again, and receive you unto myself; that where I am, there ye may be also" (John 14:2-3). This hopeful outlook permeates their pastoral care, liturgical celebrations, and daily spirituality.

Lastly, the Third Order has made significant contributions to Christological debates and discussions within the Church. Their Christology is deeply relational, emphasizing the intimate, personal relationship with Jesus Christ. By reflecting on the nature and mission of Christ, they contribute to a deeper understanding of salvation and redemption. This Christocentric approach is evident in their spiritual writings and theological reflections, drawing believers closer to the heart of the Gospel.

In conclusion, the theological contributions of the Third Order Regular are vast and profoundly impactful. They offer the Church rich insights into the Incarnation, poverty, creation, kenosis, peace, community, Eucharist, Mariology, human dignity, eschatology, and Christology. Each of these facets reflects their deep commitment to living out the Gospel in a way that is both faithful to their Franciscan roots and responsive to contemporary challenges. Through their theological reflections and practical applications, the Third Order continues to illuminate the

Key Texts and Authors

In the majestic tapestry that is the history of the Third Order Regular of Franciscans, the written word holds a place of utmost significance. Theological treatises, devotional works, and mystical writings form the cornerstone of their spiritual heritage. The array of texts and the erudition of their authors stand as an eternal testament to the depth and breadth of Franciscan thought and spirituality. These writings not only elucidate doctrinal points and spiritual disciplines but also serve as a guide for generations yearning for a closer walk with the Divine.

First among the key texts is "Admonitions" by St. Francis of Assisi. Though succinct, this compilation of exhortations encapsulates the ethos and fervent spirituality of the Franciscan way. St. Francis wrote with an urgent clarity, laying bare the virtues that ought to dominate the life of a Franciscan. Consider, for instance, his call to humility and poverty: "Blessed are the poor in spirit: for theirs is the kingdom of heaven" (Matt. 5:3). This blessed simplicity found in his writing echoes down the ages, offering clarity amid life's manifold distractions.

St. Bonaventure, known as the "Seraphic Doctor," stands as another towering figure. His seminal work, "Itinerarium Mentis in Deum" (The Journey of the Mind into God), serves as a mystical roadmap, guiding the soul through the various stages of spiritual ascent. Written in the tradition of Christian Neoplatonism, Bonaventure's text interlaces philosophical rigor with a deep, mystical yearning for God. His portrayal of the six wings of the seraph as steps towards divine union, culminating in the seventh step of contemplation, has profoundly influenced not just Franciscan spirituality but the broader Christian contemplative tradition.

The author of "The Mirror of Perfection," Brother Leo, presents yet another indispensable text. This biographical narrative sheds light on the life, deeds, and teachings of St. Francis. Authored by one of Francis's closest companions, Brother Leo's work offers unique insights into the saint's humility and simplicity. "The Mirror of Perfection" stands as an essential text in understanding the original intentions and ethos of Franciscan life. Brother Leo's firsthand accounts enrich the historical and spiritual understanding of St. Francis's mission.

Among the significant contributors to Franciscan literature is St. Bernardino of Siena, whose extensive sermons and writings have provided a robust theological foundation for the Order. His collected sermons, often classified as "sermon cycles," address a wide range of social, ethical, and spiritual issues in the context of Renaissance Italy. Bernardino's eloquence and theological depth are evident in his works where he tirelessly preached about moral reform and the spiritual rejuvenation of society.

Margaret of Cortona stands out as both a writer and a mystic. Her writings, compiled posthumously, reflect her deep penitential spirit and mystical experiences. They offer profound insights into the inner lives of saints, revealing the relentless pursuit of sanctity and divine intimacy. Her "Legenda" illustrates the transformative power of divine grace and is a testament to a life dedicated to repentance and charity.

The formidable St. Anthony of Padua, whose works and sermons have left an indelible mark on Franciscan theology, must not be overlooked. Known for his eloquence and depth, his collected sermons cover a vast array of theological topics, from the moral to the doctrinal. His exegesis on the Scriptures reveals a mind that was both deeply contemplative and pastorally engaged—a reflection of his own life's balance between eremitic solitude and zealous preaching.

Among the female voices, Clare of Assisi's "The Rule and Testament of Clare" holds a prominent place. While often overshadowed by her male counterparts, Clare's contributions are profound. Her writings underscore the Franciscan values of poverty, humility, and community life. The Testament reveals her steadfast commitment to these values, providing practical guidance for living a life dedicated to God. Clare's emphasis on the "privilege of poverty" echoes profoundly within the Order.

The "Fioretti" or "Little Flowers of St. Francis" is another enthralling text that offers anecdotal accounts of Francis and his early followers. Though the authorship remains anonymous, the text is invaluable for its portrayal of Franciscan ideals in action. These delightful vignettes capture the charming simplicity and profound spirituality of Franciscan life, embodying the joy and freedom found in absolute trust in God.

Equally important are the mystical writings of Angela of Foligno. Angela's "Liber" or "Book of Visions and Instructions" is considered a cornerstone in the literature of Christian mysticism. The work details her profound mystical encounters and provides a vivid record of her intense spiritual pilgrimage. It stands as a testament to the transformative potential of divine love and the depths of mystical union with God.

John Duns Scotus, revered as the "Subtle Doctor," crafted extensive theological works that have greatly influenced Franciscan scholasticism. His intricate explorations into the nature of being, the Immaculate Conception, and the themes of love and freedom, provide a scholastic depth to Franciscan theology. His writings, imbued with philosophical sophistication, offer profound insights into the mysteries of faith.

In more recent times, Thomas Merton, though not solely a Franciscan, brought modern relevance to Franciscan themes through his prolific writing. His works, which explore contemplative life and social justice, echo the timeless principles of St. Francis. Merton's writings bridge the ancient wisdom of the Order with contemporary issues, making spirituality accessible to modern readers.

Scriptural texts themselves play an indispensable role in the theological and spiritual writings of the Third Order Regular. The daily reading, reflection, and interpretation of the Bible profoundly shape the spiritual life and practice. From the Beatitudes to the Parables, Scripture serves as both a source and an anchor, guiding Franciscans in their quest for holiness and service. "The Lord is my shepherd; I shall not want" (Ps. 23:1) is but one example among many passages that resonate deeply within Franciscan hearts, serving as a perpetual reminder of God's provident care.

The collective wisdom found within these texts and the lives of their authors spans centuries, offering a rich reservoir of spiritual and theological insights. These writings reflect a vibrant interplay between rigorous intellectual inquiry and heartfelt devotional practice. Each work, whether it be a sermon, a mystical account, a theological treatise, or a simple admonition, contributes to the magnificent mosaic of Franciscan thought.

In conclusion, the texts and authors enumerated herein form the spiritual backbone of the Third Order Regular of Franciscans. Their contributions illuminate the path to divine union, offering both intellectual challenge and spiritual solace. Through the wisdom embedded in these writings, Franciscans and seekers alike find guidance, inspiration, and a profound sense of spiritual inheritance.

Chapter 9: Modern-Day Community Life

Amid the ceaseless march of time, the Third Order Regular Franciscans have seamlessly woven their ancient spiritual legacy into the fabric of contemporary life. In this epoch, their communities thrive as sanctuaries of prayer and service, steadfast in their commitment to the poor and marginalized. The current structure of these communities reflects an intricate balance of tradition and innovation, with members embodying the essence of their founder's vision: "Whosoever shall do the will of my Father which is in heaven, the same is my brother, and sister, and mother" (Matt. 12:50). While challenges abound in the form of secularization and dwindling vocations, these devout souls forge ahead with fortitude, guided by both gospel and Franciscan tenets. Opportunities to engage with the broader world through technological advancements present a path toward renewed evangelization, underscoring their unwavering mission: to be bearers of peace and instruments of God's love in an ever-changing society.

Current Structure and Membership

The modern-day Third Order Regular of St. Francis stands as a testament to the enduring vision of St. Francis of Assisi. In contemporary times, this order boasts a complex and spiritually rich structure, intricately designed to accommodate a diverse array of vocations, both lay and secular. This complexity is not merely administrative; it reflects a deep-seated commitment to the Franciscan ideals of poverty, humility, and service.

Members of the Third Order Regular traditionally fall into two broad categories: lay members and consecrated religious. Lay members, known as Secular Franciscans, live in the world but commit themselves to observing the principles of Franciscan life in their families and workplaces. These individuals often come together in local fraternities, fostering a sense of communal spirituality while engaging in charitable works and social justice initiatives.

The consecrated religious are bound by vows of poverty, chastity, and obedience, immersing themselves entirely in the spiritual heritage of St. Francis. These sisters and brothers live in community, dedicating their lives to prayer, ministry, and works of mercy. They serve in various capacities, such as educators, healthcare workers, and social advocates, truly bringing to life the words of Christ: "For where two or three are gathered together in my name, there am I in the midst of them" (Matt. 18:20).

The governance of the Third Order Regular mirrors the hierarchical yet collaborative spirit of its founder. At the helm is the Minister General, who, along with the General Council, oversees the global order. This leadership body is responsible for setting the spiritual and administrative direction, ensuring that all members adhere to the Rule of the Third Order Regular, which outlines their way of life. The Minister Provincial and local ministers facilitate this vision at regional and local levels, respectively.

Formation and ongoing education are crucial elements within the Third Order Regular, further binding its members in a shared journey of growth and service. The initial formation process, known as the novitiate, lasts several years and encompasses both spiritual training and practical experience in ministry. This period is pivotal, as novices discern their calling and deepen their understanding of Franciscan spirituality.

Once professed, members continue their formation throughout their lives, engaging in regular retreats, workshops, and communal studies. This lifelong learning ensures that the essence of St. Francis's teachings remains vibrant and relevant. As Romans 12:2 exhorts, "And be not conformed to this world:

but be ye transformed by the renewing of your mind, that ye may prove what is that good, and acceptable, and perfect, will of God."

The geographical and cultural diversity of the Third Order Regular today is remarkable. With communities and fraternities established on every continent, the order reflects a mosaic of human experiences and traditions. This global presence mandates a careful balance between maintaining the core Franciscan charism and adapting to local contexts. In places like Africa and Asia, the order has embraced indigenous cultures, thereby enriching Franciscan spirituality with new perspectives and expressions.

In every locale, members of the Third Order Regular strive to live out the Gospel in ways that are both contemplative and active. Their ministries often address the most pressing needs of their communities, from providing healthcare and education to engaging in advocacy for the marginalized. In this way, they emulate the compassionate heart of Christ, who said, "Inasmuch as ye have done it unto one of the least of these my brethren, ye have done it unto me" (Matt. 25:40).

The vibrancy of the Third Order Regular's modern structure is evident in its commitment to ecological stewardship, a concern deeply rooted in the Franciscan tradition. The order actively participates in various environmental initiatives, seeking to fulfil St. Francis's vision of universal kinship by promoting sustainable lifestyles and advocating for the protection of God's creation. This ecospirituality is both a reflection of the canticle of Brother Sun and an urgent response to contemporary environmental crises.

In embracing technology, the Third Order Regular navigates the fine line between modernity and tradition. Digital platforms have become invaluable tools for evangelization, formation, and community building. Online courses, webinars, and social media channels enable the order to reach broader audiences, engage younger generations, and foster a sense of global fraternity. As Pope Francis notes in "Laudato Si'", technology, when used wisely, can be a powerful means of connecting people and spreading the Gospel message.

The current structure and membership of the Third Order Regular also reflect an ongoing commitment to ecumenical and interfaith dialogue. Recognizing the importance of unity in a fragmented world, the order collaborates with other religious traditions and denominations, promoting mutual understanding and joint action in service of the common good. These efforts echo the prayer of Jesus in John 17:21: "That they all may be one; as thou, Father, art in me, and I in thee, that they also may be one in us."

Despite these strengths, the Third Order Regular faces significant challenges in today's world. Recruitment and retention of new members is an ongoing concern, as societal shifts and secularization impact vocations. Additionally, the order must navigate complex social, economic, and political landscapes, often requiring innovative approaches to ministry and community life. These challenges are met with prayerful discernment and a steadfast faith in divine providence.

Moreover, the Third Order Regular benefits immensely from the contributions of its lay affiliates. These committed men and women bring diverse talents and perspectives, enriching the order and extending its reach. Lay members often serve as vital bridges between the order and the broader secular world, embodying the Franciscan spirit in everyday contexts. Their involvement underscores the inclusive nature of the Third Order Regular, which embraces both consecrated and lay vocations as essential to its mission.

In summary, the current structure and membership of the Third Order Regular of St. Francis encapsulate a dynamic and faithful community, deeply rooted in its historical foundations yet responsive to the needs of the modern world. Through prayer, service, and continual formation, its members strive to live out the Gospel in ways that are relevant, compassionate, and transformative. Their lives bear witness to the enduring wisdom of St. Francis, who called all to follow Christ with joy and simplicity, ever mindful of the eternal promise: "But seek ye first the kingdom of God, and his righteousness; and all these things shall be added unto you" (Matt. 6:33).

Today's Challenges and Opportunities

In our contemporary age, the Third Order Regular Franciscans encounter a myriad of challenges and opportunities that shape their communal life. These issues, often complex and multifaceted, demand a steady heart and unwavering faith. For as St. Paul wrote, "We are troubled on every side, yet not distressed; we are perplexed, but not in despair" (2 Cor. 4:8). With hearts aflame with the spirit of Saint Francis, the Franciscans navigate these waters, ever anchored in their spiritual commitments.

Arguably one of the most pressing challenges today is the secularization of society. A culture increasingly indifferent or, at times, antagonistic towards religious beliefs confronts the Order. This trend makes the mission of evangelization a daunting endeavor, as the message of Christ competes with myriad distractions and secular philosophies. Yet, therein lies an opportunity. In this desert of secularism, the Third Order Franciscans can serve as an oasis of spiritual nourishment, standing as a testament to the timeless relevance of Christ's love and teachings.

The Order also faces internal challenges, particularly related to the retention and formation of new members. The call to a life of poverty, chastity, and obedience is particularly counter-cultural in an age that celebrates individualism and material success. Nevertheless, this challenge presents an opportunity to deepen the collective resolve of the community and refine its approach to formation, ensuring that new members are not only well-trained but also spiritually fortified for their lifelong journey.

Additionally, the impact of globalization cannot be disregarded. Rapid communication and mobility bring about both cultural integration and dislocation. For the Third Order Regular, this reality can pose challenges in maintaining a coherent identity amidst a flux of cultural influences. However, globalization also offers the Order a chance to foster a more inclusive and diverse community, united in their Franciscan charism while respecting cultural differences. As the Psalmist reminds us, "Behold, how good and how pleasant it is for brethren to dwell together in unity!" (Ps. 133:1).

Furthermore, social justice issues demand the attention of the Third Order Regular Franciscans like never before. The escalating conversations around inequality, environmental degradation, and human rights resonate deeply with their mission. These global issues are indeed fraught with complexity, requiring strategic and compassionate responses. Yet they also kindle the Franciscan spirit, providing a fertile ground to witness and enact the radical love of Christ. As lovers of God's creation, they can innovate sustainable ways to care for the environment echoing the words of Isaiah, "And they shall build the old wastes, they shall raise up the former desolations, and they shall repair the waste cities, the desolations of many generations" (Isa. 61:4).

The digital age, with its sophisticated technologies and social media platforms, presents another arena of both challenge and opportunity. While the constant evolution of technology can be overwhelming and potentially isolating, it also opens new avenues for evangelization and community building. The Third Order Franciscans can harness these tools to spread the Gospel, connect dispersed members, and engage with a broader audience. As Jesus instructed, "Go ye therefore, and teach all nations" (Matt. 28:19), leveraging technology can become a modern fulfillment of this divine commission.

Financial sustainability remains a perennial concern. The Order's commitment to poverty often contrasts with the necessity of maintaining their institutions and charitable programs. Economic downturns and fluctuating donations revenue can pose significant risks. However, this challenge simultaneously provides the Franciscans with an opportunity to innovate financially. Whether through social enterprises or alternative funding strategies, they can find new ways to support their mission without compromising their foundational vows.

Interfaith dialogue and ecumenical efforts are increasingly essential in today's pluralistic world. Engaging with other faith traditions requires a delicate balance of fidelity to one's core beliefs and openness to understanding. For the Franciscans, this is a call to embody Christ's love and peace, fostering relationships that transcend doctrinal differences. Engaging in genuine dialogue offers a transformative opportunity, creating channels for mutual respect and collaboration on issues of common concern.

Moreover, the lived experience of the modern-day Franciscan community includes a profound engagement with youth. The younger generation often grapples with existential questions and searches for authentic purpose. The challenge lies in presenting the Franciscan way of life as a viable and fulfilling option amid countless other paths. By mentoring and walking alongside the youth, Franciscans can illuminate the joy of a life devoted to service and simplicity, potentially nurturing the next cohort of committed members.

An essential element that remains ever-pressing is spiritual renewal. With all external challenges, the internal spiritual vibrancy of the community is paramount. The Third Order Regular must continually return to prayer, meditation, and the sacraments to draw strength. As Jesus urged his disciples, "Watch and pray, that ye enter not into temptation: the spirit indeed is willing, but the flesh is weak" (Matt. 26:41). Through regular spiritual practices, the community can rejuvenate its collective spirit, ensuring that external pursuits remain grounded in divine grace.

Lastly, the question of identity and mission continues to be vital. As societal values shift, it is crucial for the Third Order to maintain clarity regarding its core mission and identity. This requires periodic reflection and assessment, facilitated by community discussions and spiritual discernment. Therein lies the opportunity to renew their commitment to the charism of St. Francis, adapting their expressions of it to meet the needs of the time without losing its essence.

The landscape of modern-day community life for the Third Order Regular Franciscans is therefore complex yet replete with potential. By embracing these challenges with faith and creativity, the Third Order can continue to shine as a beacon of hope, carrying forth its mission with renewed vigor and unwavering commitment to the Gospel. In every trial, there gleams an opportunity to deepen faith, expand reach, and manifest God's kingdom on earth. "And let us not be weary in well doing: for in due season we shall reap, if we faint not" (Gal. 6:9).

Chapter 10: Third Order's Global Presence

The Third Order's global presence is a testament to the enduring spirit and far-reaching impact of St. Francis of Assisi's vision. With roots extending to the corners of numerous continents, the Order has not only preserved its spiritual essence but has also embraced diverse cultural tapestries, weaving them into the fabric of its mission. "Go ye therefore, and teach all nations" (Matt. 28:19) heralds their prophetic mandate, leading to an expansion that is as much spiritual as it is geographical. Whether in the bustling cities of North America, the humble villages of Africa, or the remote sanctuaries of Asia, the Franciscans' compassionate ministry resonates. Guided by a commitment to social justice, education, and environmental stewardship, they have earned a revered place in the hearts of many. Through cultural adaptations, the Order has honored local traditions while illuminating them with the Franciscans' divine light, fostering a unity that transcends borders and binds the faithful in love and service.

Expansion to Different Continents

As we delve into the majestic narrative of the Third Order's global expansion, a tale unfolds akin to the spreading of ancient olive trees, their fruitful limbs reaching out to distant lands untouched by their kind. Initially rooted in the soils of Italy under the guidance of St. Francis of Assisi, the Third Order Regular Franciscans were destined for far-reaching missions, transcending the constraints of geography and culture.

"Go ye into all the world, and preach the gospel to every creature" (Mark 16:15). These words of our Lord came alive as friars set out on their mission, bearing witness to the Gospel with zeal and humility. Their journey began humbly in the medieval towns of Europe, but the fragrant winds of the Holy Spirit soon guided their sails toward uncharted territories.

Europe served as the launching pad for what would become a global phenomenon. The earliest expansions saw the Franciscans journeying to Spain, France, and later Germany and Hungary. Each new location preserved the core values of Franciscan spirituality—poverty, chastity, and obedience— while adapting their practices to resonate with local traditions and needs. The transition was not without its challenges; language barriers and cultural differences required the missionaries to be not just evangelists but also students and scholars of humanity, embodying the teaching, "Be ye therefore wise as serpents, and harmless as doves" (Matt. 10:16).

In the 13th and 14th centuries, the Third Order began its great odyssey to the New World. Invoking the courage of Abraham embarking on his journey to the promised land, the Franciscans crossed the Atlantic, bringing the light of Christ to the Americas. These missionaries, men and women of deep faith, faced vast unknowns, bonding with indigenous populations through acts of charity and shared prayer. They founded missions that would later become towns and cities, leaving an indelible mark on the cultural and spiritual landscapes of the Americas.

An equally critical chapter unfolded in Asia. The vast and varied lands stretching from the Middle East to the Far East presented unique challenges and opportunities. The Franciscans entered regions like India and China, echoing the apostolic journeys of the early disciples. Their presence bore fruits through the establishment of churches, schools, and hospitals, contributing immensely to local societies while maintaining their commitment to the core tenets of their faith.

Africa, a continent rich in diversity and history, became another fertile ground for the Franciscan mission. Unlike the ephemeral pursuits of worldly conquerors, the Franciscans approached with a spirit of humility and service. Beginning with North Africa and later extending to Sub-Saharan regions, the Third Order members bore the torch of Christ's love through their outreach to the poor, the sick, and the marginalized.

Every new land called for a renewal of dedication and an openness to the Spirit. It was through these expansions that the Franciscans lived the Scripture: "For where two or three are gathered together in my name, there am I in the midst of them" (Matt. 18:20). Across deserts, mountains, forests, and oceans, the friars established communities rooted in fellowship and faith.

Cultural Adaptations

The Third Order Regular Franciscans, guided by the pivotal words of St. Paul, "I am made all things to all men, that I might by all means save some" (1 Cor. 9:22), have embraced the diverse tapestry of the world with an admirable grace and profound commitment. As the wind bends to the contours of the land, so have the Franciscans adapted their practices to harmonize with the myriad cultures they encounter. This chapter seeks to illuminate how these humble servants, imbued with the spirit of St. Francis, have reverently woven themselves into the cultural fabric of nations across the globe, enriching both their ministry and those they serve.

In Africa, the Third Order's presence is as deeply rooted as the ancient Baobab trees that stand as silent sentinels over the savannah. Amid the arid landscapes and vibrant communities, Franciscans have found ways to adapt their spiritual and social initiatives to the local vernacular and customs. By incorporating indigenous languages and traditions into their liturgical practices, they honor the unique spirituality of the African people while spreading the Gospel in a form that resonates deeply. The echoes of drums and the melodic harmonies of hymns sung in local dialects bear witness to a faith that transcends cultural boundaries yet speaks to the core of the human soul.

In Asia, a continent of profound spiritual heritage and rich cultural diversity, the Third Order has endeavored to understand and respect the wide array of traditions they encounter. This approach has fostered an environment of mutual respect and spiritual enrichment. For instance, in India, the Franciscans adapt their practices by engaging in interreligious dialogue and incorporating elements of Eastern spirituality that align with Christian teachings. Such efforts not only aid in the spread of the Christian message but also cultivate an atmosphere of peace and mutual understanding, reflecting the harmony preached by St. Francis of Assisi.

Latin America has long been a fertile ground for the seeds of Franciscan love and humility. Here, the adaptability of the Third Order is vividly seen through their engagement with the local communities. Festivals and celebrations, abundant in color and life, are infused with Franciscan values, creating a shared space where cultural and spiritual life blend seamlessly. The Order's commitment to social justice shines through their active involvement in advocating for the rights of the indigenous peoples and uplifting the marginalized. By aligning their missions with the local struggles, they embody the scriptural call to "defend the poor and fatherless: do justice to the afflicted and needy" (Ps. 82:3).

In Europe, where the roots of Christianity run deep, the Third Order Franciscans have revitalized their approach to align with contemporary spiritual needs. Addressing the secularization of society, they've found innovative ways to make the timeless message of the Gospel relevant and compelling. Their embrace of modern art forms, music, and digital media as tools for evangelization reveals an ingenuity that remains true to their foundational values. This creative engagement demonstrates that the spirit of St. Francis is ever vibrant, capable of speaking to the hearts of people amidst the complexities of modern life.

North America, a melting pot of cultures and beliefs, presents a unique challenge and opportunity for the Third Order. The Franciscans here have effectively navigated the delicate balance of maintaining their distinct spiritual identity while embracing the cultural diversity that defines the continent. They create inclusive spaces that welcome individuals from all walks of life, reflecting the universal call to "love thy neighbour as thyself" (Mark 12:31). Their ministries extend from urban centers to suburban neighborhoods, each tailored to meet the needs of the community they serve, from supporting immigrant families to advocating for racial justice.

In the Pacific Islands, the Third Order's cultural adaptations resonate with the gentle rhythm of the ocean waves. The Franciscans in these locales immerse themselves in the local ways of life, participating in traditional ceremonies and integrating the customs into their spiritual practices. Their presence serves as a bridge, connecting the islanders' deep spiritual heritage with the universal message of the Gospel, creating a unique symbiosis that enriches both the Franciscans and the communities they serve.

Across these diverse regions, the cultural adaptations of the Third Order reflect a profound understanding of the intrinsic connection between faith and culture. This approach is not merely about superficial changes but about a deep, empathetic engagement with the heart of each culture they encounter. Such dedication confirms the Franciscan belief that God's creation, in all its diversity, is to be revered and celebrated, echoing the words of the psalmist, "O Lord, how manifold are thy works! in wisdom hast thou made them all: the earth is full of thy riches" (Ps. 104:24).

The Franciscan ability to mold their evangelizing efforts to suit the cultural context they find themselves in is a testament to their commitment to the Franciscan charism of humility, simplicity, and poverty. By living among the people, learning their languages, and participating in their joys and sorrows, the Third Order embodies the Incarnational aspect of Christ's mission. This incarnational theology, which posits that God's presence is manifest in the ordinary and the mundane, drives the Franciscans to see each cultural adaptation not as a dilution of their message, but as a fulfillment of St. Paul's exhortation to "become all things to all people" (1 Cor. 9:22).

Ultimately, the cultural adaptations of the Third Order Regular Franciscans reveal a nuanced and respectful approach to mission work that honors the intrinsic worth of every culture. By retaining the core tenets of their faith while embracing the diversity of the world, they continue to build bridges of understanding and love. In every corner of the globe, from the bustling cities to the quiet villages, the Franciscans' presence is a living testimony to the enduring relevance of the Gospel, brought to life in myriad forms, each echoing the eternal and universal message of Christ's love.

Chapter 11: Franciscan Artistic Contributions

In the realm of artistic contributions, the Third Order Regular Franciscans have etched their legacy through works both humble and sublime, reflecting their devout spirituality and unyielding commitment to God. Their architectural masterpieces, such as the majestic basilicas and serene hermitages, invoke a sense of divine presence, where the sacred earth meets the heavens. Through literature, they have woven tales and composed hymns that echo the deep theological insights and spiritual fervor emblematic of their order, thus feeding the souls of the faithful and inspiring generations. The melodic strains of their sacred music resonate with the grandeur of the Psalms, elevating the spirit akin to King David's harp: "Sing unto him a new song; play skilfully with a loud noise" (Ps. 33:3). This fusion of artistry and faith serves not only as a testament to their dedication but also as a beacon guiding the faithful closer to the Creator, encapsulating their belief that every work, humble or grand, is an act of worship.

Architecture and Design

Woven into the very fabric of the Third Order Regular Franciscans is a profound sense of simplicity and devotion. These values are most tangibly expressed through their architecture and design. The structures built by these devout artisans are not merely physical edifices; they are, in their essence, manifestations of a sacred theology. With a focus on humility and functionality, the design reflects the Franciscan ethos, which exalts poverty, chastity, and obedience as core tenets. The vision laid out by Saint Francis of Assisi finds its echo in every stone and timber chosen for these homes of worship and community.

Consider the serene simplicity of a Franciscan chapel. A meditative space stripped of unnecessary opulence, it invites the faithful to a deeper communion with God rather than distracting with worldly grandeur. Through the delicate balance of natural light and modest adornments, the architectural design directs the heart heavenward. For "where two or three are gathered together in my name, there am I in the midst of them" (Matt. 18:20). Thus, every element serves a purpose far greater than itself, crafting an atmosphere where the divine seems almost tangible.

The intricate interplay of light and shadow in these spaces is often achieved through the use of carefully placed windows and minimalistic design. The light that pours in is akin to the very light of Christ, illuminating and sanctifying the sacred space. Such intentional design allows for moments of quiet reflection and serene prayer, creating an enduring sense of peace and reverence. It is a humble nod to the divine simplicity that Christ himself embodied during His earthly ministry.

Beyond the chapels and churches, the Franciscan commitment to simplicity and poverty can be observed in their community buildings and residences. These structures are designed to be utilitarian yet harmonious, spaces that foster the daily disciplines of prayer, work, and study. With a focus on communal living, the architectural design encourages a life of fellowship and shared purpose. Wooden beams, locally sourced stones, and simple furnishings speak to a life lived in close connection with the Earth and its Creator.

One must not overlook the role of symbolism in Franciscan architecture. The iconic Tau cross, seen often in their designs, marks a continuity with the Old Testament and signifies a life consecrated to God. "And the Lord said unto him, Go through the midst of the city, through the midst of Jerusalem, and set a mark upon the foreheads of the men that sigh and that cry for all the abominations that be done in the midst thereof" (Ezek. 9:4). This symbol serves as a silent testament to the Franciscan mission and the life of sanctification to which they aspire.

While the Franciscans may not have forged many grand cathedrals or opulent basilicas, their smaller churches and chapels have left an indelible mark on religious architecture. One profound example is the humble Porziuncola, the small chapel where Saint Francis received his divine calling. Nestled within the grander Basilica of Santa Maria degli Angeli, the Porziuncola's simplicity remains a powerful testament to the Franciscan ideal of humility. Its diminutive stature does not obscure its immense spiritual significance. This paradox of grandeur within modesty is a recurring theme in Franciscan architecture.

Gardens and outdoor spaces also play a crucial role in Franciscan architectural design. Reflecting Saint Francis's love for nature, these spaces serve as extensions of the chapel, inviting the faithful to experience God's presence in creation. Meandering pathways, secluded nooks for prayer, and simple fountains provide serene environments for contemplation and communion with the Creator. These gardens are living prayers, flourishing testimonies to a spiritual worldview that sees God's hand in every leaf and flower.

The integration of natural materials into their construction further exemplifies the Franciscan ethos of respect for creation. Stone, wood, and clay are favored for their durability and harmonic relationship with the environment. These earthly elements, shaped by skilled hands and holy intent, become vessels of divine beauty. Every stone laid and every beam set is an act of worship, a testament to a faith deeply rooted in the conviction that all creation sings the glory of God.

Franciscans have often incorporated the needs of their communities into their architectural plans. This pragmatic approach has led to the creation of multifunctional spaces that serve both spiritual and social purposes. Buildings often house libraries, dining halls, and areas for instruction, making them hubs of both spiritual and intellectual nourishment. The practical layout and accessible design reflect their mission of outreach and service, aligning with the scriptural mandate to "feed my sheep" (John 21:17).

Moreover, the Franciscan emphasis on communal life extends into their design philosophy. Often, their convents and monasteries are arranged around a central courtyard, a physical manifestation of their collective spiritual journey. These courtyards serve as sacred precincts where prayer, work, and fellowship meet. It is a layout meant to foster unity, reflecting the early Christian communities who "had all things common"

(Acts 2:44). The plain, functional lines of the architecture echo a life stripped of unnecessary distractions, allowing the focus to remain on spiritual growth and communal harmony.

In alignment with the principles of the Order, the aesthetic elements are never superfluous but hold profound meaning. Frescoes and carvings depicting scenes from the life of Saint Francis, biblical narratives, and holy symbols instruct and inspire the viewer. These artistic details, while subtle, are steeped in theological significance, echoing the teachings and visions that have shaped the Franciscan worldview. They offer visual catechesis, teaching through art what words alone cannot always convey.

Interestingly, the Franciscan contribution to architecture also includes their innovations in the use of space to enhance acoustic experiences. Music and chanting are integral parts of their worship, and many chapels are designed with acoustics in mind to amplify the harmonious sounds that rise during liturgical celebrations. This thoughtful design ensures that every note of praise is elevated, creating an atmosphere where the faithful can feel the heavenly resonance of their worship.

But what truly sets Franciscan architecture apart is the seamless blend of functionality and spirituality. These are not spaces meant to awe with their grandeur; rather, they aim to elevate the soul through their very unadorned serenity. It is a beauty marked not by opulence but by an honest reflection of the Order's vows. For just as Saint Francis himself lived a life of joyful penance, so too do these buildings stand as testimonies to lives dedicated to service, humility, and divine contemplation.

From the ancient convents that dot the Italian countryside to modern-day Franciscan institutions across the globe, the architectural legacy of the Franciscans continues to inspire. Each building is a chapter in the ongoing story of a community bound by shared spiritual ideals. "Except the Lord build the house, they labour in vain that build it" (Psalm 127:1). Thus, in every brick laid and every arch raised, the Franciscans' deep sense of divine purpose finds enduring expression.

The Franciscans' commitment to architectural and design principles steeped in their spiritual ethos offers a compelling narrative

Contributions to Literature and Music

In the realm of literature, the Third Order Regular of St. Francis has crafted a vast tapestry that speaks through the ages, not merely in words but in the souls stirred to consider the divine and the earthly together. The fusion of sacred scripture with inventive human expression has birthed works that blend the earthy passion of life with the ethereal yearnings of the spirit. Such efforts have not only evangelized and educated but have also provided solace and inspiration to countless generations.

The Order's literary contributions began with its founding figures. Their writings often took the form of epistles, hagiographies, and religious treatises. These early compositions were profound not merely for their content but for their embodiment of the Franciscan ideals of humility, compassion, and piety. Their texts were not elaborate or extravagant but bore the simplicity and sincerity reminiscent of "blessed are the meek: for they shall inherit the earth" (Matt. 5:5).

One of the most significant literary contributions from the Third Order emerged through the works of St. Bonaventure and later scholarly monks who followed in his footsteps. These thinkers and philosophers, deeply influenced by the teachings of St. Francis, strove to harmonize the wisdom of the Church Fathers with contemporary thought. The synthesis achieved in their exegeses and theological poems remained unparalleled in their time, creating a perennial wellspring for academic and spiritual inquiry.

Their prose, much like their architectural endeavors, is marked by meticulous craftsmanship and an abiding commitment to the glorification of God. As if stitching a golden thread through the tapestry of human comprehension, their words invoked a celestial resonance that found echoes in the hearts of their readers. The reflective quality of their writings insisted upon an inward pilgrimage, prompting the faithful to ponder deeply upon their relationship with Christ and His Church.

In later centuries, the Third Order continued to produce significant literary works, not just within the cloistered walls of monasteries but in the larger world, as secular and sacred literature began to intertwine more freely. Authors who imbibed Franciscan values engaged in the delicate art of storytelling, producing novels, essays, and poetry that reflected Christian virtues in nuanced and accessible ways. It was during these times, mirroring "the light of the world" mentioned in "Matt. 5:14," that the written word became a lantern guiding the faithful through the complexities of modern existence.

Beyond the written word, the Third Order has profoundly impacted the sphere of music. Perhaps no other form of art encapsulates the Franciscan spirit more profoundly than their choral and instrumental compositions. These musical offerings, often characterized by their Gregorian simplicity, served not merely to beautify the liturgy but also to elevate the soul to a state of contemplation and adoration. Much like King David's psalms, their songs and hymns were melodies intended to enrich the worship experience, invoking the Divine Presence in every note.

The cultivation of music within the Third Order came as an extension of their broader artistic aims, embodying the belief that all forms of art were avenues through which God's glory could be more fully manifest. The high call of their compositions echoed the sentiments found in "Psalms 98:4": "Make a joyful noise unto the Lord, all the earth: make a loud noise, and rejoice, and sing praise." Indeed, whether it was in grand cathedrals or humble chapels, the sanctity of these musical endeavors resonated deeply with all who heard.

Various Franciscan friars became renowned composers, merging the ancient modal scales with newer harmonic theories, thus expanding the repertoire of sacred music. Noteworthy is the juxtaposition found in their works: a blend of ancient chants and emerging polyphonic textures, each piece reflecting the prayerful, meditative stance that their founder, St. Francis, often adopted. The integration of simple melodies with complex arrangements symbolized the tension between the earthly and the divine, echoing the harmony sought in the life of every Franciscan.

This sacred music was not restricted to the confines of ecclesiastical settings. Franciscan musicians also contributed to the cultural milieu of their times by engaging with popular musical forms, enriching them with spiritually uplifting content. In so doing, they succeeded in extending the reach of their mission, embodying the exhortation found in "Ps. 150:6": "Let every thing that hath breath praise the Lord. Praise ye the Lord." Their melodies moved beyond the cloistered walls to infuse secular spaces with a touch of the ethereal.

Moreover, the marriage of text and tune in their hymnody has left an indelible impact on Christian worship worldwide. Simple yet profound, these hymns invite faithful participation, transforming congregational singing into a communal act of worship that mirrors the unity found in the Body of Christ. The Third Order's hymnal legacy stands as a testament to their unwavering devotion to fostering a prayerful spirit among believers.

The distinctive Franciscan approach to music education also warrants mention. Many Third Order institutions made significant strides in the realm of musical pedagogy, establishing schools and training choirs that upheld the highest standards of artistic excellence while infusing students with a deep spiritual ethos. These efforts not only preserved the traditional liturgical music but also inspired new generations of composers and musicians to contribute to the church's musical heritage.

Furthermore, the adaptability of Franciscan music ensured its relevance across different cultures and eras. Whether it was the incorporation of local instruments in missionary regions or the adoption of contemporary musical styles, the Third Order's versatility in music-making displayed their commitment to universality and inclusivity, hallmarks of the Franciscan charism. Their music, thus, transcends the barriers of time and place, echoing St. Francis' vision of a world united in joyous praise of the Creator.

While literature and music formed the cornerstone of their artistic contributions, the impact of the Third Order's creative endeavors extends far beyond. Their works in these realms have not merely entertained or educated but have profoundly moved the human heart toward a deeper contemplation of the Divine, fulfilling their sacred mission in every note sung and every word written. "Let the word of Christ dwell in you richly in all wisdom; teaching and admonishing one another in psalms and hymns and spiritual songs, singing with grace in your hearts to the Lord" (Col. 3:16).

In conclusion, the literary and musical contributions of the Third Order Regular of St. Francis stand as enduring legacies of their commitment to bringing forth the divine within the human condition. Their influence in these domains underscores the potential for art to serve as a bridge between humanity and divinity, leading the faithful ever closer to the heart of God.

Chapter 12: Implementing Third Order Spirituality

In delving into the practicalities of Third Order spirituality, we encounter a tapestry of personal dedication and communal engagement, woven seamlessly into the fabric of daily life. Individual spiritual practices such as contemplative prayer, fasting, and works of mercy drive us toward the heavenly vision, much like the early Christians who "continued stedfastly in the apostles' doctrine and fellowship" (Acts 2:42). Through heartfelt devotion, each member becomes a living testimony to Christ's love and the teachings of St. Francis. Community involvement, likewise, transforms the abstract into reality, breathing life into ministries that serve both soul and society. Here, the harmony of shared prayer, mutual support, and collective mission mirrors that divine call to unity and service, drawing all closer to the heart of the Gospel. Engaging in this spiritually rich lifestyle not only uplifts the individual soul but also enkindles the light of Christ within the broader world; a beacon that shines forth, proclaiming, "Let your light so shine before men, that they may see your good works, and glorify your Father which is in heaven" (Matt. 5:16).

Personal Spiritual Practices

Within the radiant tapestry of Third Order spirituality, the personal spiritual practices entrusted to the faithful are both ancient and profound. Rooted deeply in the tradition of St. Francis of Assisi, these practices are designed to draw the adherent closer to God and to embody the Gospel in everyday life. These are not mere exercises of piety, but pathways to holiness and avenues through which the divine presence permeates the soul.

One pivotal practice is the daily examination of conscience. Modeled on the life of St. Francis, who constantly sought purity of heart, this practice involves a nightly review of one's actions, attitudes, and thoughts. The examination calls for an honest acknowledgment of failures and sins, coupled with a sincere contrition and resolve to improve. "Search me, O God, and know my heart: try me, and know my thoughts: And see if there be any wicked way in me, and lead me in the way everlasting" (Psalm 139:23-24). Through this reflective dialogue with God, the soul is purified and fortified for the spiritual battles of the morrow.

Another cornerstone of personal spiritual practice is the Liturgy of the Hours. This ancient structure of prayer, also known as the Divine Office, sanctifies the segments of each day through a rhythmic cycle of psalms, hymns, and readings. These prayers bind the individual to the universal Church, echoing the angelic praises and inviting divine grace into every hour. "Seven times a day do I praise thee because of thy righteous judgments" (Psalm 119:164). For members of the Third Order, this practice not only offers structured time to commune with God but immerses them in the Sacred Scriptures, knitting their spirit to the mystic Body of Christ.

Eucharistic adoration holds a place of profound reverence in the Franciscan tradition. Spending silent time in the presence of the Blessed Sacrament deepens one's love for Christ and fosters an intimate encounter with His Real Presence. Believers are encouraged to gaze upon the Host with the eyes of faith, to meditate on the mysteries of our redemption, and to offer heartfelt thanksgiving and adoration. "O Come, let us worship and bow down: let us kneel before the LORD our maker" (Psalm 95:6). This sacred practice serves as a spiritual oasis, wherein the soul finds solace, strength, and inspiration.

Then there is the practice of scriptural meditation, or Lectio Divina, a hallmark of Franciscan personal spirituality. This slow, contemplative reading of the Holy Scriptures allows the Word of God to penetrate the heart deeply. The faithful are invited to read, meditate, pray, and contemplate—letting the Word transform their lives and guide their actions. "Thy word is a lamp unto my feet, and a light unto my path" (Psalm 119:105).

In this holy dialogue, the believer not only encounters the living Christ but is also challenged to live the Gospel more fully.

The practice of fasting and abstinence too is paramount, reminding adherents that spiritual discipline involves the body as well as the soul. Reflecting the sacrifice and simplicity that marked St. Francis' life, these practices heighten self-control and solidarity with the suffering Christ. By willingly embracing hunger, discomfort, or other sacrifices, the faithful share in Jesus' own renunciation and fortify their spirits for deeper union with Him. "But thou, when thou fastest, anoint thine head and wash thy face; That thou appear not unto men to fast, but unto thy Father which is in secret" (Matt. 6:17-18).

Furthermore, devotions to the Passion of Christ hold a special place in Franciscan spirituality. Meditating on the Stations of the Cross, praying before a crucifix, or reflecting on the Sorrowful Mysteries of the Rosary are all means by which the believer enters more fully into the mystery of Christ's suffering and redemption. "Surely he hath borne our griefs, and carried our sorrows: yet we did esteem him stricken, smitten of God, and afflicted" (Isaiah 53:4). These practices stir a profound empathy and gratitude, fostering a willingness to suffer with Christ and for others.

In addition, acts of mercy and charity are vital personal practices that embody the Third Order's spirituality. Inspired by Jesus' own example and the teachings of St. Francis, members are encouraged to actively seek out opportunities to serve the poor, the marginalized, and the suffering. "For I was an hungred, and ye gave me meat: I was thirsty, and ye gave me drink: I was a stranger, and ye took me in" (Matt. 25:35). Such acts of love extend the presence of Christ into the world, transforming both the giver and the receiver with His grace.

Silence and solitude are also integral to the Franciscan practice, drawing the soul into the divine presence away from the din of the world. Engaging in retreats, periods of silent reflection, and solitary walks in nature create sacred spaces where God's voice may be heard more clearly. "Be still, and know that I am God" (Psalm 46:10). In this stillness, the soul finds rest, renewal, and deeper communion with God, much like St. Francis did in his beloved hermitages and natural sanctuaries.

Lastly, the sanctification of daily work is emphasized in Third Order spirituality. Recognizing that all labor, when offered to God, becomes an act of worship, believers are encouraged to perform their daily tasks with diligence and joy, as offerings to the Almighty. "And whatsoever ye do, do it heartily, as to the Lord, and not unto men" (Colossians 3:23). Through this consecration of work, every moment of the day is imbued with divine purpose, and the mundane becomes a venue for grace.

Thus, in weaving these personal spiritual practices into the fabric of their daily lives, members of the Third Order aspire to follow closely in the footsteps of St. Francis, ever seeking to manifest the beauty of the Gospel. These practices serve as conduits through which the grace of God flows, shaping the soul into the likeness of Christ. They are the instruments through which a life of holiness, simplicity, and profound love for God and neighbor is actualized, bearing witness to the transformative power of a life devoted to divine pursuit.

Community Involvement

In the grand tapestry of Franciscan spirituality, community involvement stands as a cornerstone, encapsulating the essence of living in fraternity and charity. To engage with the community is to embody the love and humility that St. Francis himself so fervently espoused. "For where two or three are gathered together in my name, there am I in the midst of them" (Matt. 18:20), and it is through this sense of togetherness that the Third Order Regular manifests its spiritual ethos.

From the nascent days of the Order, the Franciscans recognized the profound importance of community. Not only as a means of mutual support but as an instrument for achieving greater goods. The Third Order's members, both secular and regular, have long sought to infuse their immediate communities with the spirit of St. Francis – a spirit of peace, simplicity, and profound love for all creation.

One cannot discuss community involvement without touching upon the myriad ways in which the Third Order has served those in dire need. Over the centuries, its members have become beacons of hope in urban slums, rural outposts, and war-torn regions. Their relentless efforts in alleviating poverty, providing education, and offering healthcare are testament to their enduring commitment to the Gospel. "Blessed are the merciful:

for they shall obtain mercy" (Matt. 5:7), and indeed, the mercy shown by the Franciscans has been both generous and transformative.

The Franciscans have often extended their arms to embrace not just those within their own folds but also those who might be considered the marginalized or the outcasts of society. In this way, they live out the words of Christ: "Inasmuch as ye have done it unto one of the least of these my brethren, ye have done it unto me" (Matt. 25:40). It is within this paradigm that the Third Order's community involvement becomes most profound, reflecting a commitment to service that transcends boundaries and defies societal norms.

The communal practices of the Third Order Regular are diverse and deeply ingrained in their daily lives. Members often gather for liturgical celebrations, retreats, and communal prayer, reinforcing the bonds that unite them. Through these shared spiritual exercises, they strengthen their collective resolve to serve both God and neighbor, creating a ripple effect that extends far beyond their immediate circles.

Moreover, the Third Order's commitment to education has fostered intellectual and moral development in countless communities. By founding schools and universities, the Franciscans have provided more than mere academic instruction. They've instilled in their students a sense of justice, compassion, and a yearning to make the world a better place. This commitment to holistic education underscores their belief in the transformative power of knowledge, emboldened by gospel values.

Holy Scripture too speaks to the significance of community, as seen in Paul's exhortation, "Bear ye one another's burdens, and so fulfill the law of Christ" (Gal. 6:2). The Third Order Regular embodies this teaching through their communal living arrangements and collaborative endeavors, showing that true spirituality flourishes in shared experience and mutual support. Their convents and friaries become sanctuaries where members can draw strength from one another, and where the collective sum is indeed greater than its individual parts.

Beyond the cloistered life, the Third Order's impact on the wider community is palpable in their numerous charitable initiatives. From running soup kitchens and homeless shelters to organizing community gardens and educational workshops, their involvement is multifarious and deeply impactful. Their actions manifest the Franciscan adage, "Preach the Gospel at all times; when necessary, use words."

The Third Order's approach to environmental stewardship is another notable aspect of their community involvement.

Inspired by St. Francis, the patron saint of ecology, members advocate for sustainable practices and engage in activities that protect God's creation. Whether through reforestation projects, clean-up drives, or educational campaigns on environmental issues, they heed the call to "replenish the earth, and subdue it" (Gen. 1:28), with a profound sense of responsibility and reverence.

Social justice, too, is a significant arena in which the Third Order exerts its influence. Rooted in the Gospel's message of equality and human dignity, Franciscans have been at the forefront of advocacy efforts for the marginalized and oppressed. Their involvement in campaigns against human trafficking, for fair labor practices, and for the protection of rights for the impoverished demonstrates their unwavering commitment to fostering a just and humane society.

Within their local parishes, members of the Third Order Regular often take on roles that bridge the gap between the laity and the consecrated life. By serving as parish administrators, catechists, and community organizers, they bring a distinctly Franciscan spirit to their roles, fostering a sense of unity and purpose among the faithful. Their presence within the parish context often serves as a tangible reminder of the broader Church's mission and the call to live out one's faith in concrete actions.

It's important to note that the Franciscans do not engage in community involvement as a mere duty or obligation. Rather, it is an intrinsic expression of their spirituality. The joy and humility with which they serve are reminiscent of the early Christian communities described in Acts, "And all that believed were together, and had all things common" (Acts 2:44). This spirit of sharing and mutual support is woven into the very fabric of their lives, making their community involvement both genuine and sustainable.

The role of lay members in community involvement cannot be understated. These individuals, inspired by Franciscan spirituality, bring their unique skills and perspectives to the mission of the Third Order. Their contributions enhance the Order's ability to adapt to the ever-changing needs of society, making their collective effort more robust and dynamic. It is a living testament to the inclusive nature of the Franciscans, who welcome varied vocations and talents.

In sum, the community involvement of the Third Order Regular stands as a living testament to their Franciscan calling. Through acts of charity, education, environmental stewardship, and advocacy, they embody the principles of their founder and bring to life the teachings of the Gospel. Their work serves as a poignant reminder of the transformative power of collective action and the enduring relevance of Franciscan spirituality in today's world. "And now abideth faith, hope, charity, these three; but the greatest of these is charity" (1 Cor. 13:13).

Chapter 13: Prayer in the Third Order

The heartbeat of the Third Order is found in its devotion to a life of prayer, which welds together the sacred and the everyday in an unceasing melody of adoration. Rich with tradition yet alive with fresh inspiration, the prayers of the Third Order span from the ancient echoes of the "Pater Noster" to the original invocations that rise from the hearts of contemporary Franciscans. These prayers encapsulate the serene wisdom and fervent faith of their spiritual forebears, melding humility with divine ardor. "Pray without ceasing" (1 Thess. 5:17), admonished the Apostle, and within the Third Order, this injunction becomes a lived reality, weaving a tapestry of daily communion with the Divine. Whether recited in the quiet solitude of a monk's cell or in the communal vibrance of a shared chapel, these supplications form the lifeblood of their spiritual journey, guiding each soul closer to the example of St. Francis, who himself embodied a life steeped in prayer and contemplation.

Traditional Prayers

Traditional prayers form the cornerstone of any spiritual journey within the Third Order Regular of Franciscans. These prayers are not mere recitations but powerful expressions of faith, humility, and connection with the divine. They have been passed down through generations, echoing the voices of countless monks, nuns, and laypersons who sought to draw closer to God through the example set by St. Francis of Assisi. In weaving a tapestry of devotion, these prayers encapsulate the very essence of Franciscan spirituality.

The daily rhythm of a Franciscan's life is imbued with specific prayers that serve to sanctify each moment of the day. From the "Office of the Hours," which structures the day into periods of prayer at morning, midday, evening, and night, to the "Angelus," a prayer that honors the Incarnation, the act of praying becomes an enduring act of worship and remembrance. "Pray without ceasing," as Paul's words in Thessalonians remind us, becomes more than an admonition but a lived reality (1 Thess. 5:17).

One hallmark of Franciscan prayer is its rootedness in humility and simplicity. The "Our Father," for instance, holds special significance, reflecting the order's close adherence to Jesus' teachings. This prayer serves not merely as a routine recitation but as a mirror on the divine simplicity, teaching the faithful to rely on God for daily bread, seek forgiveness, and strive to forgive others. "After this manner therefore pray ye: Our Father which art in heaven, Hallowed be thy name" (Matt. 6:9).

The "Hail Mary" also finds a cherished place in the daily prayers of Franciscans, echoing the reverence St. Francis himself held for the Virgin Mary. It serves as a petition for Mary's intercession, binding the supplicant to the very heart of maternal care and divine grace. The gentle repetition of "Hail Mary, full of grace, the Lord is with thee" becomes a soft mantra, guiding the soul towards spiritual contemplation and purity (Luke 1:28).

Equally pivotal are the prayers of St. Francis himself, notably the "Prayer for Peace" and the "Canticle of the Sun." The former pleads for tools of peace and instruments of God's will, embodying the Franciscan mission to be messengers of harmony: "Lord, make me an instrument of thy peace: where there is hatred, let me sow love" (Luke 6:27). The latter, the "Canticle of the Sun," expresses a profound, poetic gratitude for creation, offering praise to God for "Brother Sun," "Sister Moon," and all elements of nature, reflecting Francis' deep connection with the natural world and its Creator.

The "Divine Office," recited at canonical hours, is perhaps the most rigorous commitment for those in the Third Order. This series of prayers, psalms, and hymns brings the participant into a continual dialogue with the divine, fostering a sense of unity and shared devotion among Franciscans worldwide. "Seven times a day do I praise thee because of thy righteous judgments" (Ps. 119:164). This ongoing ritual celebrates the monastic tradition of praying at fixed hours, serving as both discipline and sanctuary.

Simplicity and communal prayer are balanced by moments of deep, personal devotion. The "Adoration of the Eucharist" remains a treasured practice, wherein members of the Third Order spend time in quiet reflection and adoration before the Blessed Sacrament. This is seen as an opportunity for intimate dialogue with Christ, echoing the words from the Holy Scriptures: "This is my body which is given for you: this do in remembrance of me" (Luke 22:19).

Furthermore, the rich heritage of Franciscan prayer includes penitential practices, especially significant during Lent. Acts of contrition and prayers seeking God's mercy mirror the humility and poverty of spirit that St. Francis exemplified. The "Act of Contrition," lamenting one's sins and promising to change, resonates profoundly within the human heart, as evidenced by the Psalmist: "Have mercy upon me, O God, according to thy lovingkindness" (Ps. 51:1).

Traditional prayers of the Third Order also extend to the remembrance of the departed. The "Office of the Dead" and the "Requiem Mass" not only honor those who have gone before us but bind the community in a collective act of hope and intercession. This ritual underscores the Catholic belief in the communion of saints and the eternal destiny each soul faces, encapsulating St. Paul's assurance, "We shall not all sleep, but we shall all be changed" (1 Cor. 15:51).

Interspersed throughout these long-established traditions are Marian prayers and feast days celebrating the lives of saints closely associated with the Third Order. These include special invocations to saints like St. Elizabeth of Hungary and St. Louis IX of France, invoking their patronage and seeking their intercession. These saints' lives serve as living prayers, their actions narrative instruments of divine mercy and justice.

In sum, the traditional prayers of the Third Order Regular stand not merely as acts of devotion but form a blueprint for living a life consecrated to God, echoing down from the days of St. Francis himself. They offer a structured path leading the devout through daily life, fostering a continuous and profound connection with the divine and community. As these prayers ascend to the heavens, they carry with them the faith, hope, and love of countless souls who have walked this path, ensuring that the spirit of St. Francis remains a vibrant, living force in the world today. "The effectual fervent prayer of a righteous man availeth much" (James 5:16).

Original Prayers

In the sacred tapestry of Franciscan devotion, original prayers hold a special place of reverence and intimacy. These prayers, often birthed from personal meditations or communal experiences, echo the profound spirituality of the Third Order Regular. Unlike the traditional prayers that have been hallowed by centuries of repetition, original prayers provide a canvas for the unique expressions of faith and longing that characterize the journey of a Third Order member.

The essence of these prayers can be traced to the humble spirit of St. Francis of Assisi, whose own prayers were often spontaneous outpourings of love and devotion. His Canticle of the Sun, for example, celebrates creation in a language that is both personal and universal. It's within this Franciscan tradition of heartfelt communication with God that the original prayers of the Third Order find their roots.

These prayers serve not just as supplications or thanksgivings, but as reflections of the collective and individual consciousness of the Franciscans. They are woven from the threads of daily life and the high ideals of their spiritual mission, creating a seamless garment of prayer that is at once simple and profound.

Consider an example of a prayer that emerged from the depths of a third-order friar's contemplation on nature. "O Lord,

Creator of the endless skies and the blooming earth, let our hearts be ever open to your wondrous works. May the beauty of your creation inspire us to live with humility and care, for 'the earth is the Lord's, and the fullness thereof; the world, and they that dwell therein' (Ps. 24:1)." Such prayers not only convey adoration but also a call to live more faithfully and harmoniously.

Often, these prayers reflect the pressing concerns and heartfelt desires of the community. During times of trial and tribulation, original prayers become a beacon of hope and trust in divine providence. In moments of joy, they burst forth in exuberant praise, capturing the spirit of communal thanksgiving.

A prayer written by a Third Order member during a period of social upheaval might read as follows: "O God of justice and mercy, in these turbulent times, grant us the strength to stand for truth and righteousness. May we be instruments of your peace in a world divided by strife. 'Blessed are the peacemakers: for they shall be called the children of God' (Matt. 5:9)." Through such invocations, the Third Order reaffirms its commitment to living out the beatitudes in a troubled world.

The act of crafting original prayers is itself a spiritual discipline. It requires the pray-er to pause, reflect, and listen for the quiet promptings of the Holy Spirit. This practice fosters a deeper connection to God, encouraging a rich, personal dialogue that is essential to the Franciscan way of life. It's in these moments of stillness and creation that the divine often speaks most clearly.

Original prayers also serve as a testament to the dynamic and evolving nature of Franciscan spirituality. They reveal how each generation of Third Order members interprets and embodies the teachings of St. Francis in their unique context. Whether addressing contemporary issues or timeless truths, these prayers are living documents of faith in action.

Imagine a prayer written in the face of an ecological crisis: "Father of all creation, forgive our neglect and greed. Help us to steward your gifts with wisdom and care. Teach us to 'walk softly upon this earth' (Mic. 6:8), that future generations may also know your handiwork." This expresses not just a plea for divine intervention but also an active commitment to change.

The original prayers of the Third Order Regular are archives of devotion that reflect their robust spirituality and serve as a conduit for divine grace. Their varied themes encompass thanksgiving, confession, intercession, and adoration, each uniquely voicing the yearnings of a communal heart bound in love and service.

In a prayer of thanksgiving, a Third Order member might intone: "Gracious God, we thank you for the gift of community, for the unseen bonds that draw us together in your love. May our lives be 'a living sacrifice, holy, acceptable unto God' (Rom. 12:1). Teach us to offer our every action as a testament to your abundance." Such prayers underscore the communal aspect of Franciscan life, emphasizing shared gratitude and collective worship.

Confessional prayers in the Third Order are marked by an acute awareness of human frailty and the redemptive power of divine grace: "Merciful Father, we confess our failures, our moments of doubt and despair. In your boundless mercy, renew our hearts and lead us once more on the path of righteousness. 'Create in me a clean heart, O God; and renew a right spirit within me' (Ps. 51:10)." This deep acknowledgment of sin paired with a hopeful plea for renewal is core to the Franciscan way of penance and conversion.

Intercessory prayers extend the reach of the Franciscan heart beyond its immediate concerns, encapsulating a global vision of charity and solidarity. For example: "Lord of infinite compassion, we lift up to you all those who suffer in body, mind, or spirit. Grant them your healing touch, your peace which passeth all understanding. 'The Lord is nigh unto them that are of a broken heart; and saveth such as be of a contrite spirit' (Ps. 34:18)."

Original prayers of adoration reveal a profound sense of awe and intimacy with the divine. Such a prayer might express: "O God of all glory, we stand in silent wonder at your presence. Every breath we take, every beat of our hearts, sings your praise. 'Bless the Lord, O my soul: and all that is within me, bless his holy name' (Ps. 103:1)." These prayers offer moments of profound connection, where the soul communes directly with God in an expression of pure love.

These original prayers, though varied in form and function, share a common foundation in the Gospel teachings and the Rule of St. Francis. They are both deeply personal and expansively communal, crafted with a reverence for tradition and a responsiveness to contemporary realities. In them, the heart of the Third Order Regular beats with a rhythm that is both ancient and ever new, drawing closer to the divine mystery through the call and response of prayer.

In conclusion, the creation of original prayers within the Third Order Regular is an act of both faith and creativity. It is a way to articulate the inexpressible and give voice to the silent yearnings of the heart. Through their words, these prayers capture the spirit of a community that seeks to live authentically according to the Gospel, to serve humbly, and to love wholeheartedly. As they rise like incense, they bear witness to a living tradition that continues to inspire and transform. For it is written, "Let my prayer be set forth before thee as incense; and the lifting up of my hands as the

Chapter 14: Hymns and Songs

Emerging from the serene valleys of Umbria and resounding through the hallowed arches of Europe's grand cathedrals, the hymns and songs of the Third Order Regular Franciscans have long been a cornerstone of their spiritual and communal life. These sacred melodies, whether plucked from the annals of centuries-old psalters or freshly penned by contemporary composers, serve as ethereal bridges connecting the faithful to the divine. The historic hymns, often imbued with the rhythmic simplicity and heartfelt fervor of their time, echo the piety and devotion exemplified by Saint Francis himself, who is said to have sung canticles even to brother sun and sister moon. In the tradition of the Psalms, "Sing unto the LORD a new song; sing unto the LORD, all the earth" (Ps. 96:1), these hymns foster communal worship and individual reflection, illuminating the path of righteousness for the brethren. Original compositions by the Third Order further enrich this heritage, breathing new life into worship with poetic lyrics and harmonious tunes that resonate deeply within the soul, embodying the message of peace, humility, and joy that is at the heart of Franciscan spirituality.

Historical Hymns

The essence of *historical hymns* within the Third Order Regular of Franciscans is deeply rooted in the confluence of faith, tradition, and spiritual expression. For centuries, these hymns have been emblematic of the Franciscan devotion to God and His creation, serving as a melodious bridge connecting the fervor of individual prayer to the collective worship of the faithful.

Hymns, in their most profound form, are not mere songs; they are vocal expressions of the divine. Among the Franciscan traditions, historical hymns play a paramount role in echoing the spiritual legacies of St. Francis of Assisi and his followers. As one reads through the annals of Franciscan history, it becomes evident that hymns like "Canticle of the Sun" and "Lauda Sion" encapsulate the order's reverence for simplicity, humility, and unwavering faith.

One of the earliest and most significant hymns attributed to St. Francis himself is the "Canticle of the Sun" ("Cantico di Frate Sole"). Written in the vernacular Umbrian dialect, this hymn reflects a profound symbiosis between creature and Creator. Drawing inspiration from Psalms, Francis praises the Lord for "Brother Sun" and "Sister Moon" and all elements of nature. It's a hymn that celebrates life in all its forms, encapsulating the

Franciscan spirit of joy and love for God's creation: "Praise ye him, sun and moon: praise him, all ye stars of light" (Ps. 148:3).

The historical trajectory of Franciscan hymns bears witness to an evolving musical and liturgical tradition. During the 13th and 14th centuries, hymns were primarily Latin chants—simple, yet profoundly spiritual. They were often sung during the Divine Office and liturgical celebrations, reinforcing the communal aspect of Franciscan worship. The use of hymns like "Lauda Sion," written by Thomas Aquinas, during the feast of Corpus Christi, integrates deep theological reflection with poetic beauty.

As the Order spread across Europe, so too did its musical footprints. Hymns formed a significant part of the Franciscan missionary endeavor, facilitating the evangelization process by introducing converts to the faith through the universal language of music. Historical records from Franciscan missions in the New World, such as those in California, indicate that hymns played an instrumental role in both liturgical rites and everyday communal life among the native populations.

The Franciscan hymnody also reflects theological currents and shifts within the Church. With the arrival of the Renaissance, there emerged a fresh wave of musical compositions. These hymns were characterized by their polyphonic structure, employing multiple vocal lines which offered a more complex and ornate style. This period witnessed figures such as Giovanni Pierluigi da Palestrina, whose sacred music compositions, though broader in focus, were greatly influenced by Franciscan simplicity and clarity of message.

In tracing the footsteps of these historical hymns, one cannot overlook the impact of the Council of Trent (1545–1563), which brought significant liturgical reforms. While the Council aimed to simplify liturgical texts and curb excesses, it also invigorated musical compositions. The hymns during this era saw a rediscovery of plainchant and a return to the more austere and contemplative forms of worship. This was resonant with the Franciscan commitment to humble and heartfelt devotion.

Moreover, the Counter-Reformation period infused Franciscan hymns with a renewed vigor and purpose. Hymns from this era often focused on penitence, forgiveness, and the ultimate hope of redemption. They served as instruments of personal and communal reflection, echoing the sentiments of Psalmist: "Create in me a clean heart, O God; and renew a right spirit within me" (Ps. 51:10). It was during this period that hymns began to be integrated into popular devotional practices, including the rosary and various litanies.

In the Baroque era, Franciscan hymnody expanded into grander compositions, aligning with the period's penchant for dramatic and emotive expression. Baroque hymns, marked by their elaborate orchestration and rich harmonies, offered a stark contrast to earlier, more solemn chants. Composers like Antonio Vivaldi, who was deeply connected to various religious orders, produced works that resonated with the Franciscan spirit of awe and wonder at the divine.

The 18th and 19th centuries witnessed further evolutions, with hymnals being printed and disseminated more widely, thanks to advancements in printing technology. These hymnals contained not just the traditional Latin hymns but also vernacular translations, making the spiritual content accessible to a broader audience. This period underscored the Franciscan mission of inclusivity and the democratization of sacred music.

The industrial era brought about a new wave of hymnodists who sought to bridge the gap between the ancient and the contemporary. This was a time of synthesis, where historical hymns were revisited, reinterpreted, and sometimes harmonized with popular tunes to encourage congregational participation. The influence of these hymns extended beyond the confines of Franciscan monasteries into parish churches and public devotional practices, reaffirming the Order's ongoing contribution to the Church's musical heritage.

In the modern era, Franciscan hymns continue to evolve, adapting to contemporary contexts while retaining their foundational ethos. Today's Franciscan hymnals reflect the multicultural and global nature of the Order. Hymns are composed not only in the traditional European styles but also incorporate African, Asian, and Latin American musical elements, reflecting the universal and inclusive nature of Franciscan spirituality. This global dimension highlights the Order's commitment to universal brotherhood and cultural adaptation.

As the world faces unprecedented challenges, contemporary hymns within the Franciscan tradition offer solace, hope, and a call to action. Modern hymn compositions frequently address themes of social justice, environmental stewardship, and peace—resonating deeply with the Franciscan charism of care for creation and the marginalized. They serve as reminders of Jesus' words: "Blessed are the peacemakers: for they shall be called the children of God" (Matt. 5:9).

The journey of historical hymns within the Third Order Regular Franciscans is a testament to the dynamic interplay between tradition and innovation. From the humble plainsong chants of medieval monastic life to the rich polyrhythms of contemporary global hymnody, these spiritual songs continue to uplift, inspire, and unite the faithful. They are, indeed, a vital part of the rich tapestry of Franciscan devotion and the ongoing narrative of their mission in the world.

Original Hymn Compositions

The sacred rhythms of the Third Order Regular Franciscans are resplendent and varied. Hymn composition, inherently a divine act, seeks both to uplift the soul and to honor the Almighty. Original hymn compositions composed by Franciscans have been a cornerstone in encapsulating the humility and reverence central to their spirituality. Singing these hymns, one can almost feel the breath of St. Francis himself, the echoes of his fervent praise resounding through time and space.

At the heart of Franciscan hymnody lies a unique approach that intertwines simplicity with profound theological insight. Composers belonging to the Third Order have consistently sought to reflect the principles of their founder, St. Francis of Assisi, emphasizing the themes of creation, peace, and brotherly love. Indeed, many of these hymns contain direct citations from Scripture, reinforcing their doctrinal solidity. "For where two or three are gathered together in my name, there am I in the midst of them" (Matt. 18:20), a verse often paraphrased or directly used in these compositions, signifies the communal aspect that is so central to Franciscan worship.

Moreover, original hymn compositions have frequently drawn inspiration from the Canticle of the Sun, one of St. Francis' own writings. Composers have taken to heart the saint's poetic language to craft melodies that celebrate the wonder of creation, the beauty of nature, and the profound peace found in divine union. Many of these hymns, though grounded in ancient inspiration, possess a timeless quality. They continue to stir the hearts of modern congregations just as they enraptured medieval franciscan communities.

The hymnic legacy of the Third Order is not merely about the past. It also encompasses contemporary works that resonate with today's spiritual challenges and joys. Drawing on the rich theological frameworks developed over centuries, modern Franciscan hymnwriters have produced works that speak to current themes like environmental stewardship, echoing "The earth is the Lord's, and the fulness thereof; the world, and they that dwell therein" (Psalm 24:1). Such themes not only honor tradition but also mobilize the faithful towards actionable faith.

In practical terms, these compositions also serve educational purposes within Franciscan circles and beyond. Lyrics rich in theological meaning provide catechetical lessons, aiding both children and adults in deepening their understanding of the faith. This aspect reflects the broader educational initiatives of the Third Order, seamlessly blending worship with teaching.

An especially notable genre within Franciscan hymnody is the Marian hymn. Given the intense devotion of Franciscans to the

Virgin Mary, it is no surprise that many original compositions center around her. These hymns often illuminate Mary's role as the "Queen of the Angels" and as the perfect disciple, encouraging the faithful to emulate her virtues. Indeed, compositions like "Ave Maria Stella Maris," which venerate Mary both as a beacon and as an intercessor, continue to be sung during liturgical celebrations and personal devotions.

Beyond the congregation, these hymns have found their way into broader realms of Christian music. Some have been adapted into different musical genres, from grand choir arrangements to simple acoustic renditions conducive for small prayer groups. The adaptability of these hymns testifies to their universal appeal and theological richness, qualities that transcend specific liturgical contexts.

An often-overlooked but critical aspect of hymn composition in the Franciscan tradition is the collaborative process. Many hymns are the result of collective endeavor—a testament to the communal ethos of the Third Order. Brother composers work closely with theologians, poets, and musicians to ensure that each piece not only glorifies God but also adheres to doctrinal soundness. This collaborative spirit imbues each hymn with a multi-faceted depth, making the final product a true labor of communal love.

Interestingly, some hymn compositions have grown out of unique historical contexts, reflecting the socio-political and spiritual climates of their times. For instance, hymns originating during periods of persecution or hardship often carry undertones of hope and resilience. These hymns have historically fortified the spirits of the faithful, acting as both a balm and a rallying cry. "The Lord is my shepherd; I shall not want" (Psalm 23:1) is a recurring theme in such works, providing solace and assurance amid trials.

Additionally, the theological contributions found within these hymns should not be overlooked. They encapsulate core Franciscan teachings in ways that are both easy to understand and deeply enriching. For example, the theme of radical humility, a cornerstone of Franciscan doctrine, finds prominent expression in many hymns. Lyrics crafted to remind the faithful of their call to humility echo the teachings of Christ and St. Francis, encapsulated in passages like "Whosoever shall exalt himself shall be abased; and he that shall humble himself shall be exalted" (Matt. 23:12).

Furthermore, the melodic structures of these hymns are designed to be easily sung by congregations of varying musical abilities. This inclusivity ensures that worship through song remains accessible to all members of the faith community, reflecting the Franciscan emphasis on communal participation.

Whether performed in grand basilicas or humble chapels, these hymns unite the community in a shared experience of faith and devotion.

Original hymn compositions continue to play a vital role in the life of Third Order Regular Franciscans, enriching their liturgical practices and buttressing their theological education. As the Order moves forward, these sacred songs remain a living testimony to their enduring commitment to living out the Gospel with simplicity and joy. "Make a joyful noise unto the Lord, all ye lands. Serve the Lord with gladness: come before his presence with singing" (Psalm 100:1-2) stands as an everlasting encouragement, echoing through the hallowed halls of Franciscan lore and practice.

This rich heritage of hymn composition offers a powerful witness to the enduring vitality of Franciscan spirituality. Each note sung, each verse penned, embodies a legacy that spans ages yet remains ever relevant, a luminescent thread in the tapestry of Divine worship.

Chapter 15: Poems of Devotion and Reflection

In the quiet alcoves of monastic life, words weave tapestries of divine yearning and contemplative grace, as meticulously as a craftsman's hand on sacred vestments. Within this chapter, we unveil a collection of poems that sing the heart's whispered prayers and the soul's earnest reflections, each verse a pilgrimage of faith and fidelity. Through the ages, from venerable tomes to modern illuminations, these poetic offerings have tenderly guided the devout on their journey to sanctity. Consider the psalmist's ancient cry, "The Lord is my shepherd; I shall not want" (Psalm 23:1), a testament to unwavering trust, echoed in every line. The poems herein crystallize moments of divine encounter and human introspection, as in "God is our refuge and strength, a very present help in trouble" (Psalm 46:1), framing the Third Order's enduring pursuit of holiness. These verses serve not merely as literary artifacts but as luminous beacons, illuminating the path of devotion that each Franciscan soul treads with earnest humility and ardent hope.

Classical Poems

In exploring the legacy of the Third Order Regular Franciscans, it is indispensable to delve into the realm of classical poems. These poetic compositions have served as profound expressions of devotion and reflection, often capturing the essence of Franciscan spirituality in a manner that prose alone could never achieve. From elegiac verses that echo the humility of St. Francis himself to epic stanzas celebrating the sacrifices and triumphs of the order's luminaries, these poems form a rich tapestry of spiritual heritage.

One of the most stirring themes found in these classical poems is the relentless pursuit of divine love. Much like how "the hart panteth after the water brooks" (Ps. 42:1), so do these poets convey an insatiable longing for God. This yearning is embodied in the meditative cadences and serene imagery that populate their works, creating a sacred atmosphere that invites the reader into deeper contemplation and prayer. Whether it is the anonymous medieval poet or the known voice of Jacopone da Todi, their words resound with an unquenchable thirst for the Divine.

The simplicity and humility championed by St. Francis are also recurrent motifs in these classical poems. The verses often eschew grandiloquent language in favor of a straightforward yet poignant diction that mirrors the Franciscan commitment to poverty of spirit. Just as St. Francis discarded worldly riches, so do these poets strip away unnecessary linguistic adornment, aiming for a pure, unfiltered praise of the Creator. This simplicity is not an absence of depth but a profound intentionality, an attempt to bare one's soul before God without pretense.

Moreover, classical poems within this tradition are rich with vivid natural imagery. St. Francis's "Canticle of the Sun" is one of the most illustrious examples, praising God through the elements of creation—Brother Sun, Sister Moon, and so forth. These poems often employ similar techniques, drawing readers into a world where every tree, river, and bird sings of God's glory. As it is written, "The heavens declare the glory of God; and the firmament sheweth his handywork" (Ps. 19:1). In this way, the natural world becomes a living testament to Divine love and artistry.

Equally compelling are the poems that delve into the notion of penance and redemption. These works do not shy away from darker themes of sin and repentance but embrace them as essential facets of the human experience. They evoke a sense of shared human frailty and the boundless mercy of God, echoing the penitential spirit found in many of the Psalms. "Hide thy face from my sins, and blot out all mine iniquities" (Ps. 51:9) could be a refrain that underpins much of this deeply reflective poetry.

In terms of structure, many of these classical poems are written in forms that were prevalent during their respective periods. The use of terza rima, couplets, sonnets, and other forms reflects the poets' mastery of their craft. Each structure is chosen with great care to best convey the weight and import of the subject matter. By adhering to these time-honored forms, the poets link their spiritual legacy to a broader literary tradition, rendering their works timeless.

The intricate dance between joy and sorrow also finds a unique expression in these poems. The Franciscans' approach to suffering is not one of avoidance but of sacred acceptance. This duality—the painful and the beautiful intertwined—mirrors the Gospel paradox that, "whosoever will lose his life for my sake shall find it" (Matt. 16:25). Here, the agony of the Cross and the glory of the Resurrection are inextricably linked, fostering a poetic exploration that is both somber and jubilant.

Prayer and meditation, key elements of the Franciscan life, are also deeply ingrained in these poetic works. The poems often read like extended prayers, dialogues with the Divine that oscillate between petition and praise. These verses become a form of lectio divina, inviting both the reader and the reciter into a holy communion through the lens of poetic contemplation. The act of reading these poems can become an act of worship in itself, a way to "pray without ceasing" (1 Thess. 5:17).

Lastly, the classical poems associated with the Third Order Regular are notable for their communal aspect. Many of these works would have been recited or sung in communal gatherings, fostering a collective spiritual experience. This communal dimension aligns with the Franciscan emphasis on fraternity and unity, reinforcing the idea that the journey towards God is one taken together, in the company of others who share the same spiritual aspirations. "For where two or three are gathered together in my name, there am I in the midst of them" (Matt. 18:20).

In summary, the classical poems within the context of the Third Order Regular Franciscans provide a multi-faceted reflection of their spiritual ethos. Through their vivid imagery, sacred simplicity, meditative quality, and communal orientation, these poetic works continue to inspire and elevate those who seek a deeper connection with the Divine. They stand as timeless testimonies to the enduring power of faith, love, and devotion—luminescent pearls in the vast ocean of Christian spirituality.

Original Poems

The beauty of poetry lies not only in its eloquence but in its ability to capture the essence of faith, devotion, and reflection in a way prose often cannot. For the Third Order Regular Franciscans, poetry is a means to encapsulate spiritual experiences and to communicate profound truths, sometimes beyond the reach of ordinary words.

Consider the following original poems crafted by members of the Third Order, each a testament to their deep connection to the divine, their dedication to living out the Franciscan charism, and their engagement with the world around them.

The Lamp of Faith

I wander through life's winding path,

Burdened by doubt, shadowed by wrath,

Yet there, amidst the firmament wide,

A flicker of hope, my faithful guide.

My soul doth yearn for heaven's light,

A beacon glowing in the darkest night,

Oh, steadfast lamp, burn ever bright,

Illuminate my way with sacred might.

No storm shall quench, no winds dismay,

The flame ignited by Christ's array,

For in His love, my faith shall stay,

A light that leads me, come what may.

In "The Lamp of Faith," the poet vividly portrays the unwavering faith of a devoted soul, who, despite life's trials, finds solace and guidance in the light of Christ. This metaphor aligns with the biblical verse, "Thy word is a lamp unto my feet, and a light unto my path" (Ps. 119:105).

Breath of Divine

A whisper from the heavens above,

A silent call, a breath of love,

In fields of grace, I roam and find,

The sacred dance of heart and mind.

Oh Breath Divine, fill me anew,

With every sigh, with skies of blue,

In stillness deep, in moments few,

I feel Thy presence, pure and true.

Whence I inhale Thy holy air,

My soul doth rise in solemn prayer,

In each exhale, release my care,

Embrace the love beyond compare.

The poem "Breath of Divine" exemplifies the intimate and personal relationship that Franciscans foster with God. Through the simple act of breathing, the poet finds unity with the divine, echoing the biblical sentiment, "And the Lord God formed man of the dust of the ground, and breathed into his nostrils the breath of life; and man became a living soul" (Gen. 2:7).

Hymn of Creation

From the morning sun to twilight's hue,

Creation sings a hymn so true,

In rivers, hills, and skies of blue,

The echo of God's love anew.

The flowers bloom, the sparrows sing,

A testament to Christ our King,

In every leaf, in every spring,

His glory shines in everything.

We join the song in voices raised,

With hearts alight, our God be praised,

In nature's splendour, ever gazed,

We see His wonder, ever amazed.

"Hymn of Creation" draws from the deep tradition within Franciscan spirituality of seeing God in all aspects of creation. This is reminiscent of St. Francis's own "Canticle of the Sun," where he praises God through Brother Sun, Sister Moon, and all elements of the natural world. The poem also brings to mind the scripture, "The heavens declare the glory of God; and the firmament sheweth his handywork" (Ps. 19:1).

Compassion's Call

In the whisper of a crying child,

In the weary face by life's trials mild,

There rings a call, so meek, so wild,

A plea for love, not reconciled.

We are the hands, we are the heart,

To heal, to bind, to mend each part,

In this divine and sacred art,

We answer Compassion's call to start.

Oh, let our deeds be prayers in motion,

A sacrament of true devotion,

With every act, with selfless notion,

We stitch the fabric of God's creation.

"Compassion's Call" serves as a heartfelt reminder of the Franciscan call to ministry and service, urging every believer to act as Christ's hands and feet in the world. This aligns with the biblical imperative, "For I was an hungered, and ye gave me meat: I was thirsty, and ye gave me drink: I was a stranger, and ye took me in" (Matt. 25:35).

Silent Prayer

In the solitude of midnight's veil,

When whispered winds begin to sail,

My heart embarks on faith's own trail,

In silence deep, where words may fail.

No voice to speak, no sound to hear,

But stillness brings my Savior near,

In sacred quiet, void of fear,

My soul in prayer, so pure, sincere.

Though earth may quake and thunder break,

In silent prayer, I'm wide awake,

With every breath, for love's own sake,

My spirit soars, heaven's view I take.

In "Silent Prayer," the poet explores the profound peace and intimacy found in quiet communion with God, a theme deeply rooted in Franciscan spirituality. This resonates with the biblical narrative of Elijah finding God in the "still small voice" rather than in the earthquake or fire (1 Kings 19:12).

Path of Humility

On pathways paved with pride's descent,

A humble heart in reverence bent,

With every step a soul's ascent,

Towards the skies where angels went.

Unburdened by the weight of self,

The humble soul finds greater wealth,

In laying down its earthly pelf,

It soars above, in heaven's health.

For blessed are the meek and mild,

In heart so pure, in spirit undefiled,

They walk with God, His tender child,

Their humble path, divinely styled.

The "Path of Humility" speaks to the core Franciscan value of humility, reflecting St. Francis's own life of simplicity and service. It evokes the beatitude, "Blessed are the meek: for they shall inherit the earth" (Matt. 5:5).

Chapter 16: Order's Relationship with Other Franciscan Orders

In the grand tapestry of the Franciscan legacy, the Third Order Regular harmoniously intertwines its journey with the manifold expressions of Franciscan spirituality. This relationship is marked by a dynamic interplay of collaboration and distinctiveness, reminiscent of the early disciples' unity in diversity. "For as we have many members in one body, and all members have not the same office" (Rom. 12:4), so too do the various branches of the Franciscan family complement and enhance each other's missions. The Third Order Regular, while steadfast in its commitment to living out the Gospel in the manner of St. Francis, often joins hands with the First and Second Orders, embarking on shared endeavors in evangelization, education, and social outreach. Each order brings its unique gifts to the communal table, fulfilling specific roles that together manifest the fullness of Franciscan charism. This symbiotic relationship ensures that the light of St. Francis' vision continues to shine brightly, illuminating paths of peace, justice, and compassion in a world ever in need of divine love.

Collaboration and Shared Missions

The Third Order Regular Franciscans have always epitomized the spirit of collaboration, not just within their own communities but also with other branches of the Franciscan family. Embodying the words of Christ, "That they all may be one" (John 17:21), these brothers and sisters have often joined forces with the First and Second Orders—The Friars Minor and the Poor Clare nuns—to further their shared mission of embodying the Gospel in action and spirit.

Instances of collaboration between the Third Order and other Franciscan Orders are as numerous as the stars in the sky. Whether working together in remote mission territories or bustling urban centers, these alliances have borne substantial fruits. From tending to the sick and feeding the poor, to educating the young and preserving the environment, the combined efforts have exemplified the Franciscan call to universal brotherhood.

A pivotal example is the joint missionary work in Latin America. The Franciscans, renowned for their zeal, have historically come together to preach the Gospel and serve indigenous populations. The Third Order Regular, with their distinctive blend of lay and clerical members, offered a unique complement to the ordained Friars Minor and the contemplative Poor Clares. These collaborative efforts not only enriched the daily lives of those they served but also fortified the bonds between the various branches of the Franciscan family.

In educational initiatives, the Third Order Regular has frequently partnered with the First Order in the founding and managing of schools and universities. Institutions like the Franciscan University of Steubenville stand as monumental testimonies to this enduring collaboration. Such educational endeavors have produced generations of students deeply rooted in Franciscan values, embodying both the intellectual rigor and the spiritual profundity of their Franciscan educators.

Yet, it is within the arena of social justice and charity work where the collaborative spirit shines most brightly. "For I was an hungred, and ye gave me meat: I was thirsty, and ye gave me drink" (Matt. 25:35). The Third Order's initiatives in social justice often see them standing shoulder to shoulder with the Friars Minor and Poor Clares, addressing societal injustices, advocating for the marginalized, and providing immediate relief for those in need. Whether it is through organized charity programs or more spontaneous acts of compassion, the impact of their united efforts is profound and far-reaching.

In environmental stewardship, the collaborative bonds have extended to global movements inspired by the teachings of St.

Francis of Assisi, the "Patron Saint of Ecology." The third and first orders often work in concert to promote sustainable living, conservation efforts, and environmental education. This shared mission echoes the Canticle of the Sun, where St. Francis praises God's creation, thereby reinforcing the interconnectedness of all life.

A remarkable feature of their collaborative missions is the complementing of distinctive roles. While the Third Order may bring a blend of lay experience and pastoral care, the Friars Minor contribute their sacramental and doctrinal expertise, and the Poor Clares offer a deep, contemplative foundation. Such synergy not only amplifies their collective impact but also enriches each order's unique charism.

In times of crisis, the cooperative efforts between the orders become a beacon of hope. Take, for example, natural disasters where different branches of the Franciscan family mobilize to provide shelter, medical aid, and spiritual comfort. The enduring crises like wars, famines, or pandemics have often seen these branches of the Franciscan family working tirelessly together, inspired by the love of Christ, to heal and restore broken communities.

Internationally, the orders join hands in ecumenical and interfaith dialogue, demonstrating that the Franciscan charism transcends boundaries. Joint initiatives in peace-building and reconciliation, especially in conflict zones, have seen the combined efforts of the First, Second, and Third Orders sowing seeds of peace and understanding among diverse populations. These efforts are informed by St. Francis's own engagement with the Sultan al-Kamil during the Fifth Crusade, highlighting the timeless relevance of dialogue and mutual respect.

The collaborative missions are not without their challenges. Differences in governance, theological perspectives, and operational strategies can pose hurdles. Yet, it is through the Franciscan commitment to humility, ongoing conversion, and mutual respect that these challenges are navigated. Just as St. Paul counseled, "bearing with one another in love; endeavoring to keep the unity of the Spirit in the bond of peace" (Eph. 4:2–3), the Franciscans have shown that unity and diversity can coexist harmoniously.

Moreover, shared spiritual practices such as joint retreats, liturgical celebrations, and periods of communal fasting and prayer reflect and reinforce the bonds between the orders. These shared moments offer a profound sense of unity and common purpose, reminding all involved that their ultimate mission is to follow in the footsteps of Christ, guided by the example of St. Francis of Assisi.

It's vital to note that these interactions also offer opportunities for mentorship and formation. Novices and young members benefit immensely from exposure to the diverse ways the Franciscan charism is lived out across the different orders. This broadened perspective enriches their vocational journey and prepares them for future roles within their communities.

Finally, as the world faces new and evolving challenges, the collaborative spirit between the Franciscan orders offers a beacon of hope and an exemplar of what can be achieved through unity and shared mission. As they continue to come together in spirit and action, they not only maintain the rich heritage passed down by St. Francis but also adapt to meet the needs of contemporary society. Their combined efforts stand as a powerful testament to the enduring relevance of the Franciscan mission in today's world.

Thus, in the bonds of collaboration and shared missions, the Third Order Regular with the First and Second Orders creates a tapestry of faith, service, and love that reflects the Kingdom of God on earth. Collaboration then is not just an operational strategy but a deep spiritual commitment to living out the Gospel in shared brotherhood and sisterhood, fulfilling Christ's own prayer for unity among His followers.

Distinctive Roles and Contributions

The Third Order Regular of Saint Francis, born in the crucible of poverty, devotion, and a radiant vision of spiritual renewal, has etched its path distinctly within the broader Franciscan tapestry. With an identity that resonates with the humble yet profound mission of its founder, the Third Order Regular remains a beacon of hope and spiritual vigor, contributing uniquely to the larger Franciscan family.

In considering the distinctive roles of the Third Order Regular within the context of the Franciscan Orders, we must reflect on the particular charisms that delineate its path. Unlike the First Order of Friars Minor and the Second Order of Poor Clares, both of which adhere to explicit forms and vows predicated on community life and cloistered spirituality, the Third Order finds its strength in the flexibility and inclusivity of its mission. It serves as a bridge, uniting laypersons with consecrated religious, facilitating a dynamic interplay between the secular and the sacred.

The Third Order Regular, by virtue of its constitution, is deeply embedded in the world while striving not to be of it. Rooted in an apostolic mission, it engages actively with society, emphasizing works of mercy, education, and social justice as manifestations of divine love and fraternal concern. This engagement is not merely an adjunct to spiritual life but an essential component of its identity, echoing the divine mandate, "For I was an hungred, and ye gave me meat: I was thirsty, and ye gave me drink: I was a stranger, and ye took me in..." (Matt. 25:35).

This order's contributions are undeniably amplified by its capacity for profound adaptation. In contrast with the comparatively static contemplative orders, the Third Order Regular embodies an adaptive spirituality, morphing to meet the exigencies of time and place while remaining steadfast to its core principles. Whether through founding educational institutions that propagate both spiritual and secular wisdom or through missionary endeavors that span the globe, the Third Order's reach has been extensive and impactful.

The members of the Third Order Regular often find themselves in environments that require both spiritual depth and practical skills. Their roles range from educators and healthcare workers to social advocates and pastoral caregivers. This versatility highlights the unique position they hold within the Franciscan family, capable of addressing a diverse array of needs while embodying the Franciscan ethos of humility and service. This adaptability and range of expertise distinguish them from their Franciscan brethren focused primarily on spiritual and communal monastery life.

Collaborative endeavors with the other Franciscan orders have only enhanced these distinctive contributions. The First Order, known for its preaching and missions, often finds support in the Third Order's educational and health initiatives. The Second Order, though more cloistered, retreats into prayer with a strengthened sense of the active support nearby, reinforcing the spiritual backbone of the Franciscans.

Furthermore, the Third Order Regular emphasizes the symbiotic relationship between action and contemplation. In this light, their distinctive role emerges in their capacity to transform contemplative insights into actionable measures, as Saint James eloquently states, "Even so faith, if it hath not works, is dead, being alone" (James 2:17). This principle informs their myriad contributions to the world and the Church alike.

The alignment of their activities with their spiritual core is strikingly evident in their environmental stewardship. Steeped in the teachings of Saint Francis, the Third Order espouses a deep reverence for creation, undertaking initiatives that not only preserve the environment but also educate others about sustainable practices. Through these efforts, the Third Order Regular integrates theological principles with real-world applications, thereby offering a holistic vision of faith in action.

This also extends to their work in social justice, where they strive to uphold the dignity of every human being. Their involvement in various humanitarian efforts around the globe speaks volumes about their commitment to the Franciscan pursuit of peace and justice. The Third Order Regular's initiatives often address systemic issues such as poverty and inequality, embodying the prophetic spirit and social consciousness that Saint Francis championed.

Their educational contributions, encompassing the establishment of schools and universities, highlight another area where the Third Order Regular stands out. These institutions not only propagate academic knowledge but also instill Franciscan values, fostering a new generation of leaders who are conscious of their moral and spiritual responsibilities. Their pedagogical approaches reflect a balance of intellect and spirituality, emphasizing integral human development.

While the Third Order's methodologies may differ from the more cloistered or itinerant Franciscan branches, their goal remains congruent—spreading the Gospel through both word and deed. Saint Luke's narrations of early Christian communities echo this harmony of faith and action, a harmony that the Third Order strives to perpetuate. As it is written, "And all that believed were together, and had all things common" (Acts 2:44), embodying this sense of unity in diversity.

The legacy of the Third Order Regular is also deeply interwoven with the lives of its saints and beati. Figures such as Saint Elizabeth of Hungary and Blessed Angela of Foligno underscore the transformative power of the Franciscan charism in personal sanctity. Their lives serve as luminous examples of how the Third Order's distinctive role can inspire profound societal and ecclesiastical contributions. Their stories emphasize that sanctity is attainable within the framework of active engagement with the world.

Moreover, modern-day Third Order communities continue to evolve, embracing contemporary challenges while maintaining their foundational mission. The integration of technology and innovative communication strategies marks a new frontier in their evangelization efforts, demonstrating their commitment to relevancy and accessibility. By leveraging modern tools, they continue to propagate Franciscan values and teachings effectively.

The Third Order Regular's relational dynamic within the Franciscan family is no mere auxiliary role but a cornerstone of its enduring strength and vitality. It exemplifies how varied expressions of a single charism can contribute to a fuller understanding and living out of the Gospel. Their unique adaptability and wide-ranging contributions affirm the order's indispensable role in the Franciscan legacy and the broader ecclesial community.

Thus, the Third Order Regular of Saint Francis reinforces the universal call to holiness and service, blending contemplative depth with active ministry. Their distinctive roles and contributions not only augment the Franciscan heritage but also illuminate pathways for ongoing relevance and spiritual rejuvenation in the ever-changing landscape of the modern world. May their example continue to inspire and guide many in the pursuit of spiritual and temporal harmony, reflecting the boundless love and wisdom of their patron, Saint Francis.

Chapter 17: Third Order's Educational Contributions

The Third Order Regular Franciscans, true to their spiritual lineage and mission, have made significant strides in the realm of education, endeavoring to illuminate minds as they shepherd souls. Their initiatives stem from the very heart of St. Francis of Assisi's vision, intertwining scholarly pursuit with profound spirituality. They pioneered the founding of schools and universities that uphold a dual commitment to academic excellence and moral virtue, embodying the scriptural tenet, "The fear of the Lord is the beginning of knowledge" (Prov. 1:7). Their educational establishments not only impart knowledge but also inculcate a sense of divine purpose, ensuring that each student perceives learning as a path to glorify God. Embracing pedagogical approaches that reflect the compassionate spirit of Christ, the Third Order emphasizes holistic education that nurtures both intellect and character. Through their enduring efforts, they have cultivated generations who are not only learned but also spiritually enriched, thus perpetuating Franciscan ideals across centuries and continents.

Founding of Schools and Universities

In the pursuit of wisdom, the Third Order Regular of St. Francis laid the cornerstone for an enduring legacy in the field of education, ensuring that their values vibrated through the corridors of numerous schools and universities. Unequivocally rooted in the vision of St. Francis of Assisi, who cherished humility and learning, these institutions arose as sanctuaries where minds were nourished, spirits uplifted, and virtues instilled.

The genesis of these educational establishments can be traced to medieval monasteries, where the members of the Third Order took upon themselves the noble task of teaching. Recognizing that enlightenment and piety must walk hand in hand, the Third Order crafted a curriculum that was a tapestry interwoven with threads of theological profundity, rigorous academic studies, and moral fortitude. These early schools stood as beacons of light in a world shrouded in feudal darkness, bearing witness to the Scripture's call: "The entrance of thy words giveth light; it giveth understanding unto the simple" (Psalm 119:130).

The foundation of universities, however, represented a grander vision. Beyond the immediate classrooms of their abbeys, the Third Order envisaged vast institutions where various academic disciplines could flourish beside theological inquiry. This vision materialized magnificently in universities sprinkled across Europe, each steeped in Franciscan tradition. They did not merely teach; they cultivated an environment where the quest for knowledge was met with the reverence of sacred wisdom.

One notable example is the role of Third Order Franciscans in the establishment of the University of Paris. Here, Franciscans lectured in subjects as diverse as philosophy, sciences, and of course, theology. They exemplified the truth spoken by the Apostle Paul to the Romans: "Be not conformed to this world: but be ye transformed by the renewing of your mind" (Romans 12:2). By fostering an educational framework that enriched both intellect and soul, the Third Order Regular Franciscans offered society nothing less than transformation.

Furthermore, the emergence of universities under their patronage underscored the Franciscans' commitment to inclusivity and social justice. They embraced students of all societal backgrounds, breaking the chains of class-bound education. With an eye toward the less privileged, they welcomed scholars who otherwise might have been relegated to lives of obscurity and servitude, reflecting the compassion of Christ who proclaimed, "Come unto me, all ye that labor and are heavy laden, and I will give you rest" (Matt. 11:28). Thus, these universities became crucibles where dreams were forged and destinies shaped, unlocking the full potential of every individual regardless of their origin.

Moreover, the Third Order's philosophy in founding universities was uniquely characterized by a Franciscan pedagogical approach. This was no dry impartation of facts, but a vibrant engagement with life itself. Students were encouraged to observe the divine in the minutiae of creation, to view their studies as part of a larger, divine tapestry. Their methodologies breathed life into the teaching of abstract concepts, transforming lecture halls into sanctified spaces where learning itself was a form of worship.

As these institutions blossomed, their reach extended far beyond the academic. Graduates carried the Franciscan ethos into various walks of life, sowing seeds of humility, charity, and scholarly integrity throughout the world. From the halls of these universities emerged theologians, philosophers, scientists, and leaders who perpetuated the flame of Franciscan ideals. Universities founded by the Third Order became the training grounds for future saints and scholars, capable of profound contributions that echoed across the annals of history.

The impact of these educational foundations remains palpable even in contemporary settings. Modern Franciscan universities continue to uphold the principles laid down centuries ago, adapting age-old wisdom to the demands of current academic and ethical challenges. They serve as enduring testaments to the vision of St. Francis and the unwavering commitment of his followers to elevate both human minds and spirits to the heights of divine understanding.

In conclusion, the founding of schools and universities by the Third Order Regular Franciscans was a monumental endeavor that has left an indelible mark on both the Church and the broader world. Their reverence for knowledge, combined with an unwavering dedication to spiritual growth, created holistically nurturing environments. It is through these hallowed halls that the eternal light of wisdom continues to shine brightly, guiding countless souls toward a higher, more enlightened path.

Pedagogical Approaches

The Third Order Regular Franciscans have long emphasized education as a pivotal element of their mission, rooting their pedagogical approaches deeply in their foundational spiritual values. These approaches, infused with a sense of divine purpose and communal salvation, were designed not just to impart knowledge but to shape virtuous lives, cultivating minds and hearts aligned with the teachings of Christ.

Central to the Franciscan educational philosophy is the integration of faith and reason, reflecting the wisdom of Solomon: "The fear of the LORD is the beginning of knowledge" (Prov. 1:7). The order's pedagogical methodologies are thus crafted to foster a harmonious balance between spiritual growth and intellectual development. Such a synthesis seeks to produce individuals who are not only academically proficient but also spiritually mature.

A distinct feature of Franciscan pedagogy is its emphasis on relational and experiential learning. The classroom, whether it be a traditional school setting or a community gathering, becomes a sacred space where knowledge is shared through relationships characterized by mutual respect and love. This mirrors the incarnational aspects of the Gospel, wherein the Word becomes flesh and truth is transmitted through proximity and encounter. Thus, the Franciscans emphasize a teacher-student dynamic akin to the relationship between Christ and His disciples, based on trust and compassionate guidance.

The Franciscans, adhering to the example of St. Francis of Assisi, promote an education that is deeply immersive and experiential. They believe that true learning extends beyond the acquisition of facts and engages the whole person in the process. Educational activities often include hands-on experiences, community service, and direct engagement with the natural world. This is reminiscent of Christ's parables, which drew upon everyday life to reveal profound truths, an approach encapsulated in the teaching, "Consider the lilies of the field, how they grow; they toil not, neither do they spin" (Matt. 6:28).

Moreover, the parallel drawn between the learners' growth and their increasing involvement in service to others is a hallmark of Franciscan pedagogy. The Franciscans teach that education should lead to action, particularly in the service of justice and mercy. Hence, their pedagogical methods frequently incorporate social action projects, encouraging students to apply their learning in tangible ways that reflect Christ's call to "love thy neighbour as thyself" (Matt. 22:39). This approach not only facilitates cognitive development but nurtures a sense of moral responsibility and social accountability.

Another critical aspect of Franciscan education lies in the fostering of a contemplative and reflective mindset. Educators in the Third Order encourage learners to regularly engage in self-examination and prayer, nurturing an inner spiritual life that provides the foundation for external actions. This practice mirrors the Biblical exhortation to "Be still, and know that I am God" (Ps. 46:10). By cultivating such an interiority, Franciscans aim to produce students who are not only knowledgeable but also wise and discerning.

In line with the holistic nature of their educational goals, Franciscan pedagogy also places a strong emphasis on the communal and collaborative aspects of learning. The educational processes in Franciscan institutions are therefore characterized by an inclusive and participatory spirit, where dialogue and shared experiences are central. This fosters a sense of fraternity and mutual edification reminiscent of the early Christian communities described in the Acts of the Apostles: "And all that believed were together, and had all things common" (Acts 2:44).

The Franciscans' educational approach also extends to the use of the arts as vehicles for learning and spiritual enlightenment. They recognize the inherent power of beauty to uplift the human spirit and draw it closer to God. Incorporating music, visual arts, and drama into the curriculum is not merely to develop aesthetic appreciation but to deepen the encounter with the divine. This is echoed in the divine creation narrative where the beauty and goodness of God's work are evident: "And God saw every thing that he had made, and, behold, it was very good" (Gen. 1:31).

In the realm of academic inquiry, the Third Order promotes a rigorous but humble pursuit of truth. They acknowledge the limitations of human understanding and the mystery inherent in divine revelation. Thus, their pedagogy encourages a scholarly humility that respects both revelation and reason. This epistemic humility aligns with the scriptural wisdom that "the wisdom of this world is foolishness with God" (1 Cor. 3:19), inviting students to a lifelong quest for understanding tempered by faith and reverence.

Franciscan educational settings also focus on fostering personal development and self-discipline. Structured routines, communal living, and shared responsibilities are used to teach the virtues of diligence, patience, and perseverance. This disciplined environment, however, is infused with a spirit of kindness and encouragement, reflecting Paul's exhortation to the Philippians: "Let your moderation be known unto all men. The Lord is at hand" (Phil. 4:5). By balancing discipline with compassion, Franciscan pedagogy strives to produce individuals of strong moral character and spiritual depth.

To support the educational journey, the Third Order places significant importance on mentorship and pastoral care. Teachers and mentors are not just instructors but spiritual guides who accompany students on their path of learning and spiritual growth. This relational approach reflects the shepherd-like care Christ showed to His followers, as noted in the Gospel of John: "I am the good shepherd, and know my sheep, and am known of mine" (John 10:14). Through personalized attention and spiritual mentoring, Franciscans aim to nurture both the intellect and the soul.

One cannot discuss Franciscan pedagogy without highlighting its adaptability and responsiveness to cultural contexts. The Franciscans have consistently demonstrated a capacity to engage with diverse cultures and societal challenges, adapting their educational approaches to meet the unique needs of the times and places they serve. This flexibility is rooted in their deep commitment to the Gospel's transformative and inclusive vision, as proclaimed by Paul: "There is neither Jew nor Greek, there is neither bond nor free, there is neither male nor female: for ye are all one in Christ Jesus" (Gal. 3:28). Embracing this universal message, Franciscan education seeks to be a beacon of hope and unity in an ever-changing world.

Ultimately, the pedagogical approaches of the Third Order Regular Franciscans stand as a testament to their enduring commitment to holistic education. By integrating the spiritual, intellectual, communal, and experiential dimensions of learning, their educational philosophy aims to cultivate individuals who are not only knowledgeable but also virtuous, compassionate, and committed to serving God and humanity. In this spirit, the Franciscans continue to illuminate the path of learning with the light of faith, dedicated to the divine wisdom that guides all true understanding.

Chapter 18: Health Care and Social Services

In their unyielding pursuit of Christ's compassion and mercy, the Third Order Regular Franciscans have tirelessly devoted themselves to the care of the sick and the downtrodden, embodying the words of our Lord Jesus: "Inasmuch as ye have done it unto one of the least of these my brethren, ye have done it unto me" (Matt. 25:40). Their journey began with the founding of hospitals and care homes, where the sick were not only treated with medical aid but also with the love and dignity they so richly deserve. Over the centuries, these Franciscan institutions blossomed into havens of hope and redemption, standing as beacons of light in times of plague and poverty. Beyond the physical healing, the Franciscans extended their mission through diverse social programs, including shelters for the homeless, food distribution networks, and educational outreach for the marginalized. Their contributions have left an indelible mark on society, echoing the eternal message of charity and love as taught by St. Francis of Assisi. With hearts ablaze with the spirit of service, they exemplify a living gospel, a testament to the enduring power of faith in action.

Founding of Hospitals and Care Homes

The establishment of hospitals and care homes by the Third Order Regular of St. Francis stands as a testament to their unwavering commitment to the Gospel and love for humanity. From their earliest days, the Franciscans embraced the call to serve the sick, the poor, and the marginalized. The inspiration stemmed directly from their founder St. Francis of Assisi, who revered the words of Christ: "Inasmuch as ye have done it unto one of the least of these my brethren, ye have done it unto me" (Matt. 25:40).

Early Franciscans recognized that providing physical care went hand in hand with spiritual support. Embodying a holistic approach to health, they saw the divine in every person they served. This profound realization led to the founding of some of the first hospitals and care homes in Europe. The Franciscans' commitment to this mission underscored their belief that every act of service was an act of worship and love towards God.

The genesis of these institutions can be traced back to the 13th century. It was during this period that Franciscan friars began to establish infirmaries within their monasteries. These humble beginnings were marked by limited resources, but they were rich in compassion and dedication. The infirmaries were intended not just for members of their order but for any soul in need. This inclusiveness was a radical departure from the practices of many contemporary institutions, which often restricted access based on social status or ability to pay.

Building on these foundations, the Franciscans expanded their efforts across Europe. In Italy, Spain, and France, they founded hospitals that became renowned for their care. They addressed not only physical ailments but also the spiritual and emotional needs of patients, offering a unique blend of care that was innovative for its time. Narratives from these hospitals are replete with stories of miraculous recoveries and profound transformation, all attributed to the compassionate, faith-driven care provided by the friars. St. Bonaventure keenly described the act of healing as participating in God's redemptive work, echoing, "He healeth the broken in heart, and bindeth up their wounds" (Ps. 147:3).

By the 14th century, the Franciscans' commitment to healthcare had evolved into a more structured system. One of the most significant developments was the establishment of specialized care homes for the elderly, orphans, and those suffering from leprosy and other chronic diseases. These institutions were often attached to monasteries and were funded through alms and donations. The friars and nuns running these facilities viewed their work as an extension of their spiritual vows, serving not only the body but also the soul.

One notable example of a Franciscan-founded institution is the hospital of St. Mary of the Angels in Assisi. This hospital became a beacon of hope for the local community and beyond. Patients received comprehensive care, including prayer, medical treatment, and spiritual counseling. Records from this period reflect the holistic nature of the care provided, demonstrating the Franciscans' commitment to treating the whole person, inspired by the biblical injunction to "Bear ye one another's burdens, and so fulfil the law of Christ" (Gal. 6:2).

In the following centuries, the model established by the early Franciscans spread throughout the Christian world. Europe saw a proliferation of hospitals bearing the mark of the Franciscan approach. These institutions became centers of medical innovation and compassionate care, often leading advancements in medical treatment and pastoral care. The Franciscans' pioneering work laid the groundwork for modern healthcare institutions, which today still echo the principles of holistic care and charity.

Vital to the success of these hospitals and care homes were the Franciscan sisters who dedicated their lives to this mission. Orders of nuns such as the Sisters of St. Clare, founded by St. Clare of Assisi, played a crucial role. These committed women worked tirelessly alongside the friars, providing nursing care, managing hospital operations, and ensuring that the spiritual and physical needs of every patient were met. Their work personified the principle found in Proverbs: "She stretcheth out her hand to the poor; yea, she reacheth forth her hands to the needy" (Prov. 31:20).

During times of crisis, such as the various plagues that swept through Europe, the Franciscan hospitals and care homes became sanctuaries of hope and healing. Stories abound of Franciscans who, rather than fleeing the cities, ran towards the plague-stricken areas to offer help. They ministered to the sick and dying at great personal risk, embodying the ultimate form of Christian charity. The selflessness of these individuals was widely recognized, and their efforts frequently recorded in both religious and secular accounts, serving as a testament to their faith and dedication.

Beyond Europe, the Franciscans carried their mission to the New World and Asia. They established hospitals and care homes in the Americas and Asia, continuing their centuries-old tradition of compassionate care. In the New World, particularly in Latin America, the Franciscans were instrumental in founding hospitals that served both the indigenous population and the European settlers. The efforts in these regions were marked by a deep sense of respect and cultural sensitivity, learning from and incorporating local healing practices into their care methodologies.

The legacy of these early Franciscan hospitals and care homes is still evident today. Their influence can be seen in the numerous hospitals and medical institutions around the world that continue to operate under the Franciscan ethos. These modern institutions strive to uphold the same principles of compassionate care, holistic treatment, and spiritual support that were the hallmarks of the original Franciscan foundations. The seeds planted by the early Franciscans have borne fruit in ways that would have made St. Francis himself proud, compelling us to remember, "And the King shall answer and say unto them, Verily I say unto you, Inasmuch as ye have done it unto one of the least of these my brethren, ye have done it unto me" (Matt. 25:40).

The Franciscan commitment to the founding of hospitals and care homes reflects a profound integration of faith and service. It is a testament to their understanding of Christ's teachings and a powerful reminder of the enduring impact of their mission. As we look back on their monumental contributions, we are called to recognize the sacredness of caring for one another in both body and spirit, echoing the timeless teachings of the Gospel.

Social Programs and Outreach

The Third Order Regular of St. Francis has always been a beacon of hope and light, committing itself tirelessly to the service of the most vulnerable among us. Their social programs and outreach efforts, reflecting the profound compassion of their founder, St. Francis of Assisi, have not only contributed to the alleviation of immediate suffering but also to the transformation of entire communities. Following Christ's mandate to "love thy neighbour as thyself" (Mark 12:31), these programs have become an enduring testament to the Franciscan ideals of humility, charity, and simplicity.

The cornerstone of Franciscan outreach lies in their unyielding commitment to the poor and marginalized. Rooted deeply in the admonition of the Gospel "Inasmuch as ye have done it unto one of the least of these my brethren, ye have done it unto me" (Matt. 25:40), the Third Order Regular has pioneered various initiatives aimed at addressing social inequities. This unassuming yet powerful devotion often translates into feeding the hungry, sheltering the homeless, and providing clothing to those in need. But beyond just meeting physical needs, their programs delve into offering hope, dignity, and a sense of belonging to those who society has often neglected.

In the crowded alleys and bustling slums of urban metropolises, one finds Franciscans engaged in outreach programs that uplift entire communities. Frequently, they establish soup kitchens and food banks which serve as lifelines to countless individuals and families. In these places, the poor find nourishment not just for their bodies, but for their spirits, as they are welcomed with a warm smile and a listening ear. Nor is this ministry confined to the cities; in rural areas, Franciscans bring aid to those isolated by distance and circumstance, ensuring that no soul is beyond the reach of their loving care.

Education is another pivotal aspect of the Franciscans' outreach. With the belief that empowering individuals through knowledge can break the chains of poverty, countless educational initiatives have been launched. Schools have been established in impoverished areas, providing quality education to children who would otherwise have no access. These institutions are often beacons of hope, turning slums into schools and children into scholars. Franciscan educators also emphasize moral and spiritual formation alongside academic learning, thus nurturing well-rounded individuals who embody the virtues of faith, hope, and charity.

The Franciscans' outreach is not confined solely to material assistance. They also place significant emphasis on mental and emotional support, recognizing the holistic nature of human needs. Through counseling services, support groups, and community-building activities, they foster environments where individuals can heal from trauma, overcome addictions, and regain a sense of purpose in life. Echoing the words of Jesus, "Come unto me, all ye that labour and are heavy laden, and I will give you rest" (Matt. 11:28), these services offer solace and sanctuary to weary souls.

Medical outreach programs are another critical facet of Franciscan social services. Rooted in the tradition of caring for the sick, Franciscans have founded numerous clinics and mobile health units to provide essential medical care to underserved populations. These services include not only basic health check-ups and treatments but also preventive measures and health education, aimed at empowering communities to maintain their own well-being. The healing ministry of the Franciscans echoes the Gospel's call to "heal the sick, cleanse the lepers, raise the dead, cast out devils: freely ye have received, freely give" (Matt. 10:8).

The Franciscan approach to social programs and outreach is also characterized by an unwavering commitment to justice and advocacy. They take an active stand against systemic injustices that perpetuate poverty and inequality. This includes involvement in campaigns for land rights, fair wages, and sustainable development. Franciscans work alongside the oppressed, vocalizing their grievances and championing their rights in various public and political arenas. Their advocacy is deeply anchored in the conviction that every individual is created in the image of God and deserves to live in dignity and peace.

Furthermore, the Franciscans have initiated numerous programs aimed at environmental stewardship, recognizing the intrinsic link between social justice and the natural world. They understand that environmental degradation disproportionately affects the poor and work diligently to promote sustainable practices. Community gardens, reforestation projects, and environmental education sessions are just some examples of their efforts to care for "our common home" as Pope Francis articulated in "Laudato Si'". This commitment underscores the prophetic vision of St. Francis, who saw all creation as a reflection of the Creator's love.

The Franciscan Third Order's outreach extends beyond geographic and cultural boundaries. Globally, they have established missions in various countries, adapting their programs to meet local needs. Whether it's combating human trafficking in Southeast Asia, providing clean water in Africa, or rebuilding war-torn communities in the Middle East, their presence is both a sign and instrument of God's love and mercy. Truly, the words of Isaiah resonate within their work: "And the

Lord shall guide thee continually, and satisfy thy soul in drought, and make fat thy bones: and thou shalt be like a watered garden, and like a spring of water, whose waters fail not" (Isa. 58:11).

Partnerships and collaborations with other organizations, both secular and religious, amplify the impact of Franciscan outreach programs. These alliances enable them to pool resources, share expertise, and reach a wider audience. Through interfaith and ecumenical efforts, they build bridges of understanding and cooperation, working together to serve humanity's collective needs. This spirit of collaboration aligns with the biblical call for unity in service: "And if one prevail against him, two shall withstand him; and a threefold cord is not quickly broken" (Eccles. 4:12).

Volunteers play a crucial role in the execution of social programs and outreach activities. Lay Franciscans, local community members, and partners from other walks of life often come together in a spirit of mutual aid and solidarity. These volunteers, inspired by the Franciscan values, offer their time, skills, and resources to support various initiatives. Whether it's a young student helping in a food distribution center or a retired professional providing pro-bono services, their collective efforts embody the teaching, "Let us not be weary in well doing: for in due season we shall reap, if we faint not" (Gal. 6:9).

Ultimately, the Social Programs and Outreach of the Franciscan Third Order Regular are a living manifestation of St. Francis' vision of a world transformed by love and service. Through their tireless work, Franciscans remind us that the Kingdom of God is not an abstract ideal but a tangible reality brought about by acts of mercy and justice. In their hands, the Gospel comes alive, and in their hearts, it finds relentless expression. As they continue to offer themselves in service to others, they inspire all who encounter them to emulate their example and to join in the divine mission of healing and hope.

The legacy of Franciscan outreach is one of profound and eternal significance, revealing the heart of God in every act of kindness they perform. It is through these humble yet mighty deeds

Chapter 19: Significant Historical Events

Throughout the centuries, the Third Order Regular of St. Francis has borne witness to numerous significant historical events that have shaped its mission and identity. From its inception in the thirteenth century, under the vision of St. Francis, whose call to live the Gospel in radical simplicity reverberated across a spiritually turbulent medieval Europe, to the profound impacts of the Protestant Reformation and the Council of Trent, which necessitated a recalibration of its apostolic activities, the Order has met adversities with grace and resilience. During the industrial revolution, the push for social justice and the establishment of numerous educational and healthcare institutions served as beacons of hope in a rapidly changing world. In more recent times, the transformative experience of the Second Vatican Council, encapsulated in the call for renewal and engagement with the modern world, further invigorated the Order's commitment to evangelization and service. As Scripture reminds us, "And let us not be weary in well doing: for in due season we shall reap, if we faint not" (Gal. 6:9). Each historical milestone, marked with trials and triumphs, subtly weaves the intricate tapestry of a tradition that remains steadfast in its pursuit of peace, humility, and fraternity.

Major Milestones

The passage of centuries has witnessed a tapestry of major milestones within the Third Order Regular of St. Francis of Assisi. Each epoch, marked by divine inspiration and human endeavor, resonates with the call to embody Christ's teachings. The Third Order Regular commenced with St. Francis of Assisi's revolutionary vision, carving out a path distinct from the secular world while remaining worldly in its mission—serving the poor, comforting the sick, and educating the uninformed.

The canonization of saints from within the Third Order stands as testimony to the divine favor and solemn dedication of its members. St. Elizabeth of Hungary, canonized in 1235, epitomized the virtues of humility and charity, dedicating her life to the care of the impoverished and sick. Her deeds remind us, "Let your light so shine before men, that they may see your good works, and glorify your Father which is in heaven" (Matt. 5:16).

Another momentous occasion occurred in 1246 with the approval of the Rule of the Third Order by Pope Innocent IV. This formal recognition gave structure and legitimacy, fostering a unified identity among the diverse groups adhering to Franciscan precepts. The promulgation of the Rule not only codified spiritual and communal life but also facilitated the expansion of the Order's mission.

The 14th century saw the rise of Blessed Angela of Foligno, whose mystical writings and deep spirituality earned her a revered place within the Order and Church history. Her spiritual journey, full of divine revelations and internal struggles, exemplifies the transformative power of divine grace, echoing the words of Paul, "My grace is sufficient for thee: for my strength is made perfect in weakness" (2 Cor. 12:9).

The founding of the Franciscan University of Steubenville in 1946 marked another historic milestone. This institution has since become a beacon of Franciscan education, merging academic rigor with spiritual formation. Its impact is felt not only in its intellectual contributions but also in the spiritual revival it has sparked among its students and faculty. Through the university, the Third Order Regular has significantly influenced contemporary Catholic higher education.

One cannot overlook the profound influence of the Second Vatican Council (1962-1965) on the Third Order. The council's emphasis on returning to the sources of Christian faith and renewing religious life inspired a deep introspection and revitalization within the Order. The decree "Perfectae Caritatis" called for adaptation and renewal of religious life according to the spirit and purposes of founders, leading to a rejuvenation of Franciscan charisms.

The global expansion of the Third Order Regular, particularly during the 19th and 20th centuries, signifies yet another critical milestone. From Europe to the Americas, Africa, and Asia, the Order has planted seeds of faith, hope, and charity across continents. This period of expansion reflects the fulfillment of Christ's command: "Go ye therefore, and teach all nations, baptizing them in the name of the Father, and of the Son, and of the Holy Ghost" (Matt. 28:19).

The 2000s ushered in the digital age, and with it, new methods of evangelization and communication. The Third Order embraced these technologies to spread its message, creating online communities and virtual prayer networks. Such initiatives demonstrate the Order's adaptability and commitment to meeting the needs of contemporary society, proving that while the medium may change, the message remains timeless.

In 2009, the declaration of St. Louis IX of France as the patron saint of the Third Order Regular was a significant spiritual milestone. St. Louis, a king renowned for his justice and piety, embodies the harmonious balance of secular authority and spiritual humility. His life reminds members of the Order that leadership and sanctity are not mutually exclusive but are, in fact, complementary paths to serving God's kingdom.

Parallel to these joyous occasions, the history of the Third Order Regular is punctuated by challenges and resolutions that have shaped its evolution. The Black Death of the 14th century devastated communities but also demonstrated the Order's resilience and unwavering commitment to mercy and care for the afflicted, embodying the call to "love thy neighbor as thyself" (Mark 12:31).

In conclusion, the major milestones of the Third Order Regular paint a vivid portrait of a community rooted in faith, continually evolving through divine grace and human perseverance. From the canonization of saints to global expansion and the embrace of modern technology, each milestone marks a significant chapter in the ongoing story of Franciscan spirituality. As we reflect on these accomplishments, we are reminded of the enduring relevance and vitality of the Third Order Regular, ever striving to "walk worthy of the vocation wherewith ye are called" (Eph. 4:1).

Challenges and Resolutions

In the chronicles of the Third Order Regular Franciscans, the story of triumph is often interwoven with threads of trials. These trials, though daunting, had a purifying effect, testing the faith and resolve of its members. Indeed, as James the Apostle reminds us: "My brethren, count it all joy when ye fall into divers temptations" (James 1:2). The history of this Order, akin to gold purified in the furnace, stands testament to the divine providence that guided them through storms, always steering them back to their holy mission.

One of the earliest and most substantial challenges was securing papal approval for the Third Order itself. In its inception, the hierarchical structure of the Church was less accommodating to new, unconventional forms of religious life. It took perseverance and countless appeals before the Order's unique mission and vision received ecclesial endorsement. This development, while arduous, ultimately fortified the Order's foundation, enabling it to stand resiliently against future tribulations.

Furthermore, the Order faced internal dissensions, arising from varied interpretations of St. Francis's vision. As the Order expanded, so did discrepancies over the strictness of the Rule. Such conflicts threatened to fracture the unity, yet, they were resolved through a series of General Chapters and consultations with influential theologians and canonists. These measures ensured uniformity in practice and interpretation, adhering closely to the foundational principles laid by St. Francis.

External threats also loomed large. During periods of political upheaval and anti-clerical sentiment, Franciscans were at times persecuted. In some regions, they were forced into hiding, and their properties were seized. Yet, these trying times became a testament to their unwavering faith. They drew strength from the words of the Apostle Paul: "For when I am weak, then am I strong" (2 Cor. 12:10). Their underground networks and covert missions kept the flame of their spirituality alive, even in the darkest times.

Perhaps one of the most poignant challenges was their outreach and mission work in foreign lands. Confronted by unfamiliar cultures, languages, and sometimes hostile environments, the Franciscans endeavored to spread the Gospel. Many missionaries faced martyrdom; others grappled with the immense difficulties of adaptation and evangelization. In these moments of extreme adversity, the Order's reliance on divine grace became paramount. Their missionary zeal, driven by the Great Commission ("Go ye therefore, and teach all nations" (Matt. 28:19)), led to numerous conversions and the establishment of thriving Christian communities.

Financial constraints consistently presented a significant challenge throughout their history. Maintaining their missions, educational institutions, and charitable programs required substantial resources. The Order's vow of poverty compounded these difficulties, compelling them to rely heavily on donations and almsgiving. Yet, through the grace of God and the beneficence of supporters, these financial hurdles were often overcome at the eleventh hour, reinforcing the belief in divine providence.

Disease and plague, too, cast long shadows. The Franciscan commitment to care for the sick and the poor placed them on the frontlines during outbreaks of plague and other epidemics. Many lost their lives serving others, embodying the scriptural call to love one's neighbor as oneself (Mark 12:31). Their sacrifice not only alleviated the suffering of countless individuals but also fortified the Order's reputation as steadfast servitors of humanity.

Adaptation to changing societal norms posed another intricate challenge. As the world advanced, so did its complexities, often clashing with the Order's traditional values. The waves of secularism, individualism, and materialism lapped at the shores of their communities. In response, the Order continually engaged in theological reflection and discourse, seeking to reconcile contemporary issues with their deeply-rooted spirituality. This adaptive resilience enabled them to remain relevant and impactful even amidst rapid societal transformations.

One illustrative resolution to these modern challenges was their incorporation of technology into their ministry and outreach programs. Initial resistance gave way to the realization that digital platforms could serve as effective tools for evangelization and community building. The establishment of online forums, digital prayer groups, and virtual educational courses allowed the Order to reach a broader audience, thus fulfilling their mission in a contemporary context.

Moreover, the Third Order faced significant challenges during times of doctrinal disputes within the Church. Maintaining orthodoxy while addressing new theological questions demanded profound wisdom and discernment. Through persistent dialogue, engagement with Church councils, and the guidance of illustrious theologians within their ranks, the Order effectively navigated these turbulent waters. Their contributions to theological discourse often served as bridges, harmonizing faithfulness to tradition with intellectual integrity.

Environmental stewardship became another pivotal arena of challenge and resolution. As ecological crises intensified, the Franciscan commitment to "Brother Sun and Sister Moon," inspired by the Canticle of the Creatures, necessitated actionable advocacy for the environment. The Order endorsed and promoted initiatives that stressed the harmonious coexistence of creation and humanity, thereby addressing ecological sins and fostering a spirit of stewardship reflective of their founder's teachings.

The Third Order was not immune to the challenges posed by political shifts and changing power structures. At times they found themselves navigating delicate waters where their missions and values might collide with political agendas. The resolution of such challenges often required the diplomatic acumen of their leaders, who worked tirelessly to protect their communities and missions while remaining true to their principles. These prudent negotiations frequently illustrated the wisdom drawn from Christ's exhortation to be "wise as serpents, and harmless as doves" (Matt. 10:16).

In recent history, the challenge of vocational crises emerged as one of the most pressing. With fewer individuals choosing religious life, the Order had to grapple with sustaining its initiatives and legacy. Responding to this, the Order adopted renewed vocations programs, emphasizing the beauty and sanctity of a life dedicated to service and spirituality. These efforts, focused on the youth and facilitated through retreats, seminars, and personal testimonies, sought to reignite the flame of vocations in the modern age.

Amidst all these challenges, the unwavering commitment of the Third Order Regular Franciscans to their foundational charisms – poverty, humility, and love for all creation – served as their guiding light. Time and again, their ability to remain steadfast in faith and adaptable in action enabled them to surmount the hurdles placed before them. In their trials and tribulations, elegies turned into paeans of praise, for it is written, "They that wait upon the LORD shall renew their strength; they shall mount up with wings as eagles; they shall run, and not be weary; and they shall walk, and not faint" (Isa. 40:31).

Chapter 20: Third Order and Vatican II

In the light of the Second Vatican Council, the Third Order Regular of St. Francis found itself immersed in a sweeping renewal, affirming both its ancient charism and contemporary relevance. The Council's impetus for aggiornamento, or updating, resonated deeply within the Third Order. They embraced the spirit of revisiting foundational principles, delving into the essence of Franciscan poverty, humility, and love for creation. As it is written, "Let us not love in word, neither in tongue; but in deed and in truth" (1 John 3:18). Thus, members sought to rekindle their commitment to live out the Gospel in practical service and visible unity with the Church's mission. This period marked an era of introspection and action, where statutes and practices were meticulously examined, fostering a deeper communal prayer life, renewed liturgical participation, and an invigorated presence in educational and social spheres. The synthesis of tradition and modernity propelled the Third Order into a dynamic force, perpetually harmonious with both the spirit of St. Francis and the transformative vision articulated in the Council.

Impact and Changes

The sacrosanct assemblies of the Second Vatican Council (1962-1965) heralded monumental shifts across the ecclesiastical landscape, none more transformative than those witnessed within the Third Order Regular of Franciscans. The Church, in its divine wisdom, sought renewal and rejuvenation through aggiornamento, a term denoting both updating and a return to the ancient sources. As in all sectors of the Church, the Third Order Regular underwent significant metamorphosis, blending the ancient with the contemporary, thus embodying the essence of Vatican II's spirit.

Before the council, the Third Order Regular lived a life often defined by a strict adherence to prescribed patterns of spirituality and apostolic work. Their ways, though profoundly rooted in the Franciscan charism, were bound by formalism. Post-Vatican II, new avenues opened, urging Franciscans to engage more directly with the world's pressing and evolving needs. "Behold, I make all things new" (Rev. 21:5) came to life as the Franciscans embraced shifts not merely in liturgical practice but also in their missional outreach and social justice endeavors.

One of the most palpable impacts was the shift towards a decentralized mode of governance and local autonomy. No longer were communities bound solely to directives from a central authority but encouraged to discern and address the specific spiritual and material needs germane to their locale. This democratization came with the growing emphasis on collegiality and subsidiarity, principles profoundly asserted during the council. The Third Order, hence, saw a burst of localized initiatives that catered precisely to the diverse communities they served.

Liturgical reform also formed a cornerstone of the Vatican II impact, creating waves throughout the Third Order Regular. The Novus Ordo Missae, promulgated by Pope Paul VI, ushered in profound liturgical changes. The use of the vernacular in the Mass and other liturgical expressions made the sacred mysteries more accessible to the laity, thereby deepening their participation. For Third Order Franciscans, this meant leading more inclusive and engaging liturgical celebrations that resonated with the faithful's everyday language and experience. The liturgy, no longer distant and foreign, became a bridge to the divine love that St. Francis ardently preached.

Furthermore, there was an invigorated focus on the scriptural foundations of the faith. "For whatsoever things were written aforetime were written for our learning" (Rom. 15:4). Franciscans, always regarded as lovers of Holy Scripture, found renewed impetus in Vatican II's Dei Verbum to intensify their biblical scholarship and preaching. The Franciscan emphasis on living the Gospel simply but profoundly was revitalized, reinforcing the authenticity and relevance of their spiritual witness in an ever-modernizing world.

Expanded social engagements were another pivotal transformation. Gaudium et Spes, the Pastoral Constitution on the Church in the Modern World, called the Church to recognize and respond to the signs of the times. The Third Order's ministries began to embody this call by actively participating in socio-political spheres, advocating for human rights, ecological stewardship, and global peace. This was a departure from their previous focus which was often more cloistered and limited in scope.

Educational and catechetical methods evolved as well. The council advocated for a more profound understanding of faith, which necessitated a shift from rote memorization to active engagement and understanding. Franciscan educators and catechists were summoned anew to cultivate an informed laity, capable of integrating faith with reason and living out their vocation in the secular world. This meant developing new curricula that fostered critical thinking and a deeper comprehension of the faith's mysteries.

One aspect that cannot be overlooked is the emphasis on ecumenism propagated by Vatican II, most notably through the decree Unitatis Redintegratio. The Third Order Regular, embodying the simplicity and humility of their founder, became agents of reconciliation and dialogue with other Christian denominations and indeed with other faiths. The unity Christ prayed for in John 17:21—"That they all may be one; as thou, Father, art in me, and I in thee"—became a tangible mission, promoting interfaith understanding and cooperation.

The Franciscan charism of living in poverty, identifying with the marginalized, and advocating for the downtrodden gained new layers of interpretation and action post-Vatican II. The preferential option for the poor, as emphasized in various council documents, called Franciscan communities to reassess their involvement in social justice and direct service. Programs targeting homelessness, unemployment, and systemic inequality gained ground, seeing the Third Order Franciscans become visible champions of the oppressed.

Even the daily life and fraternal habits within communities saw transformations. A renewed emphasis on communal discernment and shared decision-making processes helped in fostering unity and mutual respect among members. These changes were not merely structural but rooted deeply in the desire to return to the fraternal spirit of St. Francis, who envisioned a brotherhood founded on love, humility, and service.

The Vatican II call to holiness for all the baptized encouraged individual members of the Third Order to pursue sanctity through their unique vocations and contexts. This was not a passive, abstract holiness, but an active, engaged pursuit of perfection in everyday life. Lay members saw their roles not as secondary to the clergy but as vital parts of the Church's mission, deserving spiritual formation and opportunities for leadership.

Technological advancements, embraced post-Vatican II, aided the Franciscans' outreach programs. Mass communication tools such as television and radio were supplemented by burgeoning digital platforms, facilitating wider evangelization efforts. The Third Order Regular used these means to preach Gospel values, extending their influence and offering spiritual support to a global audience. The increased adoption of these technologies aligned with the council's endorsement of modern means in the service of the Gospel.

Vatican II's emphasis on the universal call to mission also resonated deeply with the Third Order. The decree Ad Gentes necessitated a more aggressive and expansive missionary zeal. Franciscans rekindled their missionary heritage, spreading the Gospel to new frontiers, be it through establishing missions in remote regions or engaging in contemporary missionary activities like social media evangelization.

In summary, the transformative impact of Vatican II on the Third Order Regular Franciscans is profound and multifaceted. It revitalized their spiritual life, missionary zeal, and social engagement, urging them to adapt ancient principles to contemporary needs without losing their core Franciscan identity. This alignment with the council's decrees facilitated a renewed and vibrant expression of their charism, continuing to inspire devotion and service in a rapidly changing world.

Contemporary Practices

The Second Vatican Council, convened between 1962 and 1965, marked a pivotal moment in the history of the Roman Catholic Church, bringing profound changes that reverberated through its various institutions, including the Third Order Regular of Saint Francis. The Council's call for renewal and aggiornamento—an Italian term meaning "bringing up to date"—encouraged the Third Order to examine and reinvigorate its practices in light of the contemporary world. This chapter explores the ways in which the Third Order has adapted its customs, devotional practices, and community life to the post-Vatican II era while remaining deeply rooted in Franciscan spirituality.

The spirit of Vatican II propelled the Third Order to recontextualize traditional practices, making them more accessible and relevant to modern believers. One of the key reforms was the shift from Latin to vernacular languages in liturgy and prayer. This change significantly enhanced the communal prayer experience, making the words of the Divine Office and Mass more comprehensible and spiritually nourishing to members. Consequently, the Liturgy of the Hours, long a cornerstone of Franciscan prayer life, saw a revitalized participation among the faithful, fostering a communal sense of unity and purpose.

Equally significant was the renewed emphasis on the laity's role within the Church, a central theme of Vatican II. The Third Order Regular, originally founded to provide laypeople with a means to live out Franciscan ideals in their daily lives, found a fertile ground in this renewed focus. Contemporary practices now encourage broader lay participation in various apostolic missions and community activities. Members, both ordained and lay, collaborate more closely, sharing responsibilities in evangelization, educational initiatives, and social justice efforts, thus embodying the Council's vision of a more inclusive Church.

The commitment to social justice has always been a hallmark of Franciscan identity, echoing Christ's own ministry to the marginalized. Post-Vatican II, the Third Order has expanded its social justice efforts, advocating for systemic change as well as offering direct aid. For instance, modern-day Franciscans are often at the forefront of movements supporting immigrants, addressing issues of climate change, and campaigning for economic justice. These initiatives can be seen as an extension of the Sermon on the Mount's beatitudes, encouraging the faithful to "hunger and thirst after righteousness" (Matt. 5:6).

Educational reform also came to the forefront as the Third Order responded to Vatican II's calls for engagement with the world. Many Franciscan institutions began to emphasize an education that integrates spiritual formation with academic excellence. A renewed curriculum often includes studies in eco-theology, social ethics, and interfaith dialogue, reflecting broader horizons and a deeper understanding of global issues. Such an integrative approach ensures that graduates are not only academically proficient but also spiritually grounded, ready to serve as compassionate leaders in a complex world.

Another critical aspect of contemporary practice is interreligious dialogue. Vatican II's declaration on the relation of the Church to non-Christian religions, Nostra Aetate, encouraged the pursuit of common ground with other faith traditions. The Third Order has embraced this directive, engaging in meaningful dialogue and collaboration with various religious communities. These efforts are not merely academic but often result in joint social and environmental initiatives, aiming to reflect the Franciscan values of peace and brotherhood across cultural and religious divides.

The spiritual renewal prompted by Vatican II also called for a closer examination of personal and communal prayer life. Contemporary Franciscans dedicate significant time to contemplative prayer, inspired by St. Francis's own mystical experiences. Practices such as Eucharistic adoration, silent retreats, and the promotion of lectio divina—an ancient method of prayerful scripture reading—have seen a revival. These practices encourage deep personal encounters with Christ and enhance communal bonds among members.

A notable modern development is the expanded use of technology in evangelization and community building. The Third Order has adapted to digital platforms to reach broader audiences. Social media, podcasts, and virtual prayer meetings enable Franciscans to connect with people beyond geographic limitations, offering spiritual guidance and fostering a global community united by shared faith and values. Importantly, these tools are used not merely for outreach but for fostering genuine spiritual engagement and community connection.

Community life has also been enriched by contemporary practices that encourage greater inclusivity and fraternity. Modern Franciscans often live in smaller, more flexible communities that emphasize shared responsibilities and mutual support. This shift reflects a return to the simplicity and humility advocated by St. Francis, creating environments where members can live out their vocations more authentically and joyfully.

The emphasis on living simply and fraternally is not limited to communal settings but extends into personal lifestyle choices. Many Franciscans today commit to sustainable living practices, reflecting a deep respect for creation as articulated in Pope

Francis's encyclical Laudato Si'. Their efforts range from community gardens to renewable energy initiatives and reducing waste, integral expressions of their ecological spirituality.

In terms of spiritual direction and ongoing formation, there is a renewed emphasis on mentorship and accompaniment. Experienced members guide newer ones through individualized spiritual guidance, retreats, and structured formation programs. These programs are designed to deepen one's understanding of Franciscan theology and spirituality, while also addressing contemporary issues such as mental health and social media ethics, ensuring that the Third Order continues to be relevant and supportive.

In conclusion, the Third Order Regular of Saint Francis has not merely survived the monumental shifts brought by Vatican II but has thrived, finding new ways to embody and express its timeless mission. By adapting its practices to contemporary contexts while staying true to its foundational charism, the Third Order remains a vibrant and dynamic force within the Church and the world. As they continue to "preach the Gospel to every creature" (Mark 16:15), today's Franciscans are a living testament to the enduring relevance of their spiritual heritage.

Chapter 21: Vocations and Formation

The path to joining the Third Order Regular is a journey both profound and transformative, one that begins with a stirring call from the heart that echoes the words of Isaiah, "Here am I; send me" (Isa. 6:8). The process is meticulously structured, balancing spiritual fervor with disciplined formation. Prospective members embark on an initial period of discernment, a time consecrated to prayer, reflection, and guidance from seasoned friars. This is followed by a novitiate phase, steeped in the teachings of St. Francis of Assisi, where novices immerse themselves in communal living, study, and charitable works. The formation continues with postulancy, where deeper theological training and practical service cultivate the virtues necessary for this sacred vocation. This elaborate journey refines the soul, aligning it with the divine calling to a life of poverty, chastity, and obedience. "And be not conformed to this world: but be ye transformed by the renewing of your mind" (Rom. 12:2), the Apostle Paul's exhortation, comes alive in this process, ensuring that each member emerges not merely as a follower of St. Francis but as a torchbearer of his timeless mission.

Process of Joining the Order

The process of joining the Third Order Regular of St. Francis begins with an individual discerning a divine calling. This inner voice, often soft yet insistent, draws one toward a life of poverty, chastity, and obedience. "For many are called, but few are chosen" (Matt. 22:14). The path often starts with engagement in the local community's spiritual and social activities, allowing the aspirant to taste the Franciscan way of life in its essence. This initial stage is informal but crucial, providing the space for contemplation and prayerful consideration.

Prospective members, known as aspirants, initially enter a phase called postulancy. This period, usually lasting six months to a year, allows them to live alongside the community and fully participate in its daily routines. During this time, they adopt the habit of prayer and work, immersing themselves in the spirituality and mission of the Order. The Gospel's words come vividly alive: "Whosoever will come after me, let him deny himself, and take up his cross, and follow me" (Mark 8:34). Aspirants receive guidance from a spiritual director, aiding in personal reflection and vocational discernment.

Following postulancy, if both the aspirant and the community discern a genuine calling, the individual then proceeds to the novitiate phase. This stage, often one year in duration, serves as an intensive period of spiritual formation and theological education. Novices delve deeper into the charisms of St. Francis, studying the sacred texts, the lives of saintly figures, and particularly the rule of the Third Order Regular. It's a transformative time, a crucible where the novice's faith is tested and refined: "But he knoweth the way that I take: when he hath tried me, I shall come forth as gold" (Job 23:10).

The world outside may see the novitiate as a retreat from its busy chaos, but within, it is a rigorous journey of the spirit and mind. Novices engage in community activities, worship, and service – from caring for the destitute to environmental stewardship, reflecting the myriad facets of Franciscan life. The immersion grows deeper, and they learn the spirit of fraternity, simplicity, and humility. Yet, this period is also one of self-examination, laying bare one's inner essence, much akin to the parable of the prodigal son, who returns home with a contrite heart: "I will arise and go to my father, and will say unto him, Father, I have sinned" (Luke 15:18).

Upon completing the novitiate, a significant milestone arrives: the profession of temporary vows. These vows of poverty, chastity, and obedience are taken for a limited period, often three to six years. They signify a profound commitment and incorporate the novice fully into the community while still allowing for further discernment. Temporary professed members, now called simply professed friars or sisters, continue their formation, balancing theological study with hands-on ministry. Symbolically and practically, they begin to embody the teachings: "And he that taketh not his cross, and followeth after me, is not worthy of me" (Matt. 10:38).

During these years of temporary profession, members further integrate into the life of the Order, undertaking various apostolates and missions. They spread the Franciscan gospel through evangelization, education, and social justice initiatives, becoming living witnesses to the faith. This phase is akin to the scriptural journey from Egypt to the Promised Land, a time of trials and triumphs, as they seek to embody the virtues and mission of St. Francis. "For I know the thoughts that I think toward you, saith the Lord, thoughts of peace, and not of evil, to give you an expected end" (Jer. 29:11).

When the period of temporary vows concludes, the journey culminates in the profession of perpetual vows. Here, the individual forever dedicates their life to the principles of the Third Order Regular, making a total and unreserved commitment to the life of evangelical counsels. This solemn vow is a covenant with God, witnessed by the community, a profound act of faith echoing the Scripture: "And whatsoever ye do, do it heartily, as to the Lord, and not unto men" (Col. 3:23). The community joyfully welcomes the permanently professed member into the fullness of its fellowship.

The profession ceremony is both joyous and solemn. In a ritual bathed with prayer, psalms, and hymns, the member professes their vows before the altar, receiving a symbolic embrace from the community. This culminating moment is richly steeped in liturgical beauty and poignancy, embodying the divine mystery of vocation. "For the kingdom of heaven is like unto a man that is an householder, which went out early in the morning to hire labourers into his vineyard" (Matt. 20:1). The journey, though formally concluding with perpetual vows, transitions into a lifelong path of ongoing formation, reflecting an ever-deepening commitment to Franciscan spirituality.

Throughout their life, the professed members continually engage in ongoing formation, seeking to grow in holiness and fidelity to their vocation. This commitment encompasses continuous spiritual, intellectual, and pastoral development. Enriched by retreats, spiritual exercises, and advanced theological study, their mission and ministry evolve. They are beacons of divine light, continually replenished and refocused: "Thy word is a lamp unto my feet, and a light unto my path" (Ps. 119:105). Their journey underscores the lifelong dynamic of learning and transformation.

The contours of this holy voyage, though structured, are dynamically touched by divine grace and individual zeal. Practicing discernment and humility, they embrace the totality of Franciscan life, embodying the words of St. Francis: "Preach the Gospel at all times and when necessary, use words." The process of joining the Order is profoundly personal, yet communal, echoing the shared journey of faith and mission. It is a pilgrimage marked by steps of faith, acts of love, and vows of devotion, leading each member nearer to the heart of Christ.

Training and Ongoing Formation

The call to the Franciscan life is a divine invitation that beckons souls to a profound journey of transformation and devotion. The training and ongoing formation of those who answer this call is not merely an initial instruction but a lifelong pursuit, resonating with the echoes of Christ's own path. It involves constant nurturing of the spiritual, intellectual, and communal aspects of one's life in the Order.

Formation in the Franciscan tradition illuminates the path to holiness, much like the journey of Abraham who "went out, not knowing whither he went" (Heb. 11:8). It is both a crucible and a comfort, shaping individuals through the manifold experiences of community life, prayer, and service. The process begins with a harmonious blend of spiritual guidance and practical instruction, deeply rooted in the teachings of St. Francis of Assisi.

Novices entering the Third Order Regular embark on an initial period known as postulancy. This stage, typically lasting several months, introduces the aspirants to the demands and joys of Franciscan life. Guided by spiritual mentors, they immerse themselves in the Rule of the Third Order, which offers a roadmap for living out the evangelical counsels of poverty, chastity, and obedience.

Essential to the formation process is the novitiate, a more intense period of spiritual and communal training. During this time, novices retreat into a reflective and contemplative space, akin to Jesus' own retreat into the wilderness. Here, they delve deeper into the mysteries of the Franciscan charism, participating in daily Mass, the Divine Office, and other communal prayers. The words of St. Paul ring true: "For bodily exercise profiteth little: but godliness is profitable unto all things, having promise of the life that now is, and of that which is to come" (1 Tim. 4:8).

The novitiate is not solely a time for personal reflection but also a period for building strong fraternal bonds. The novices, now clad in the simple yet profound habit of the Order, learn the value of living in community, embracing the essential virtues of humility, simplicity, and fidelity. They partake in communal activities and manual labor, following the example of St. Francis, who saw work as a means of living out the gospel.

Upon completing the novitiate, and having discerned their vocation, novices make their temporary profession of vows, committing themselves to the Franciscan way of life for a specific period. This temporary commitment allows for continued growth and discernment. The vow of poverty, for instance, challenges them to rely wholly on God's providence, mirroring the lilies of the field that "toil not, neither do they spin" (Matt. 6:28). Chastity transforms their relationships, directing their affections towards divine love. Obedience humbles them, aligning their wills with God's greater plan.

During this period of temporary vows, the friars engage in further theological studies and practical ministerial training. They are prepared for the diverse ministries they will undertake, from pastoral care to educational endeavors. Their academic formation is rigorous, rooted in Sacred Scripture and the rich Franciscan intellectual tradition. This intellectual pursuit gives them the knowledge and wisdom required to "give an answer to every man that asketh you a reason of the hope that is in you" (1 Pet. 3:15).

Formation does not conclude with the solemn profession, for it is a way of life that is perpetually unfolding. Lifelong learning and spiritual growth are cornerstones of the Franciscan journey. Solicitous of this continuous growth, the Order provides opportunities for ongoing formation. Regular retreats, workshops, and study sessions are organized to keep the friars spiritually nourished and intellectually sharp, allowing them to adapt to new challenges and continue their mission with zeal and insight.

Community life remains at the heart of ongoing formation, for the bonds of brotherhood forged in initial formation are to be strengthened continually. This living together in unity serves as a testament to the Psalmist's proclamation: "Behold, how good and how pleasant it is for brethren to dwell together in unity!" (Ps. 133:1). Through mutual support and shared responsibilities, the friars grow in charity and learn to bear each other's burdens, thus fulfilling the law of Christ.

In addition to communal support, spiritual direction remains an essential aspect of ongoing formation. Regular meetings with a spiritual director help the friars to discern God's will in their daily lives, to address personal challenges, and to deepen their relationship with Christ. This guidance ensures that their spiritual fervor does not wane but rather, like the wellspring of living water, continues to flow abundantly and refreshingly.

Moreover, the Franciscan commitment to service means that the friars are frequently engaged in new ministerial contexts. These diverse experiences, whether in parishes, schools, hospitals, or missions, require continual adaptation and learning. The Order supports this by providing specialized training that equips the friars with the skills necessary to meet the demands of their specific ministries effectively and compassionately.

Indeed, the Franciscan education extends beyond the boundaries of theology and philosophy. Practical skills, from healthcare to environmental stewardship, are also imparted, ensuring that the friars can respond to the needs of the world with competence and compassion. This holistic approach to formation resonates with the words of Micah: "What doth the Lord require of thee, but to do justly, and to love mercy, and to walk humbly with thy God?" (Mic. 6:8).

Not neglecting the importance of personal spiritual practices, the formation process also encourages the development of a rich interior life. Daily meditation, the rosary, and other devotions are integral to sustaining the friar's spiritual well-being. This private prayer life complements the communal aspects of worship and service, fostering a deep, personal communion with God that is the wellspring of all Franciscan activity.

Finally, the Franciscan formation is universal yet deeply personal. Each friar's journey is unique, and the training and ongoing formation process respects this individual vocation. Through a balanced approach that integrates spiritual, intellectual, and practical dimensions, the Franciscans cultivate well-rounded individuals capable of witnessing to the Gospel in diverse and impactful ways, truly becoming instruments of God's peace in a world often wrought with turmoil.

As we reflect on the depth and breadth of Franciscan training and ongoing formation, we recognize it as a dynamic and life-long commitment to following Christ in the spirit of St. Francis.

It is a continuous journey of becoming, marked by transformation and growth, deeply rooted in tradition yet responsive to the needs of the contemporary world. This formation guides the Franciscan friars to embody the prayer of St. Francis, "Lord, make me an instrument of thy peace," as they go forth to serve the Church and the world.

Chapter 22: Ecumenical and Interfaith Efforts

In the spirit of St. Francis's profound love for all creation and his unwavering commitment to peace, the Third Order Regular has undertaken significant ecumenical and interfaith efforts, fostering a landscape of dialogue and cooperation that transcends human divisions. Rooted in the Scripture, "Blessed are the peacemakers: for they shall be called the children of God" (Matt. 5:9), these endeavors aim to build bridges across diverse faith traditions while nurturing mutual understanding and respect. Whether through shared initiatives with other Christian denominations or collaborative projects with different faith communities, the Franciscans have been at the forefront of creating spaces where the divine spark in every individual is acknowledged and celebrated. These harmonious pursuits not only enrich the spiritual tapestry of the Church but also manifest the Gospel's call to love one's neighbor as oneself (Matt. 22:39), reflecting a resilient commitment to unity in a fractured world.

Dialogue and Cooperation

The Third Order Regular Franciscans have long embraced the call to dialogue and cooperation with other religious traditions and Christian denominations. This mandate is deeply rooted in the vision of St. Francis of Assisi himself, who saw all of creation as a unified whole under the providence of God. It is an epic journey through time and contemplation, a journey that sees barriers dissolve in the presence of divine love. St. Francis, with a heart emboldened by divine charity, reached out to Muslims during the Crusades, embodying the biblical exhortation, "If it be possible, as much as lieth in you, live peaceably with all men" (Rom. 12:18). This profound sentiment has echoed down the centuries, finding new resonance in the lives and works of those who have committed themselves to the Third Order Regular.

Through the practice of dialogue, the Third Order has sought to build bridges of understanding and peace, seeing in every person the image of Christ. Cooperation with other faiths is not merely a strategic endeavor but a sacred duty, an extension of the Gospel's call to love thy neighbor. These efforts are colored by an ecumenical spirit that values both unity and diversity, resonating with the call to be peacemakers. "Blessed are the peacemakers: for they shall be called the children of God" (Matt. 5:9). In the spirit of this beatitude, Third Order Franciscans have been active participants in interfaith councils, fostering mutual respect and understanding.

Significant milestones in interfaith dialogue have often been accompanied by tangible actions of cooperation. Whether it is participating in joint humanitarian missions or engaging in theological conversations, the aim has been consistent: to witness to the truth while honoring the richness of diverse traditions. In regions torn by conflict, Third Order Franciscans have often stood as beacons of hope, working hand-in-hand with communities of various faiths to promote peace and healing. These collaborative efforts serve as modern-day expressions of the Good Samaritan parable, reminding us that mercy knows no boundaries.

A noteworthy example of such cooperation can be found in the shared initiatives between the Franciscans and other monastic traditions, such as the Benedictines and the Jesuits. These partnerships have produced a wealth of knowledge, particularly in areas of social justice and ecology, reflecting the shared commitment to stewarding God's creation. "The earth is the Lord's, and the fullness thereof; the world, and they that dwell therein" (Ps. 24:1). Joint conferences, academic exchanges, and combined efforts in social programs serve to highlight the underlying unity of purpose that transcends denominational lines.

Moreover, interfaith dialogues have not been limited to Christian denominations alone. The Third Order has engaged in fruitful discussions with Jewish, Muslim, Buddhist, and Hindu communities. These interactions, often held in the spirit of mutual search for truth, have paved the way for greater understanding and respect. Shared values such as compassion, peace, and justice form the bedrock of these dialogues, reaffirming the belief that truth can be found across the spectrum of religious experience. As Proverbs aptly states, "Wisdom is the principal thing; therefore get wisdom: and with all thy getting get understanding" (Prov. 4:7).

The essence of dialogue is the spirit of listening. The Franciscans have learned that true dialogue involves an openness that goes beyond mere tolerance. It involves a deep listening, an empathetic engagement with the other's narrative. This kind of listening echoes the biblical call to "Be swift to hear, slow to speak, slow to wrath" (James 1:19). It transforms encounters into moments of grace where hearts and minds may be opened to new vistas of understanding.

One of the transformative stories of dialogue and cooperation is the ongoing relationship between the Third Order Franciscans and the Islamic community in different parts of the world. This relationship, initiated by the historic encounter between St. Francis and the Sultan of Egypt, continues to bear fruit today.

Modern Franciscans have participated in numerous interfaith events, leading to initiatives that address common social concerns, such as poverty and refugee crises, thus embodying the scriptural adage, "Bear ye one another's burdens, and so fulfil the law of Christ" (Gal. 6:2).

Theological exchange forms another crucial aspect of these dialogues. By exploring theological and philosophical questions together, Franciscans and their dialogue partners enrich one another's understanding of the divine. These exchanges are often characterized by their respectful tone and intellectual rigor, seeking to illuminate rather than to win arguments. Topics such as the nature of God, ethics, and the human condition are discussed not to assert dominance but to draw closer to the divine mystery that transcends all human comprehension.

In settings where religious tensions run high, the Third Order's commitment to dialogue and cooperation has often acted as a stabilizing force. Their presence in such contexts is a testament to their faith in peace and reconciliation, mirroring Christ's work of breaking down "the middle wall of partition" (Eph. 2:14). These courageous acts of bridge-building go beyond diplomacy; they embody the Gospel's radical message of universal brotherhood.

Equally important is the Third Order's involvement in educational initiatives that aim to bridge gaps and foster mutual understanding. Joint educational projects with other religious communities, seminars on comparative theology, and collaborative research projects have all been avenues to further this mission. Education, seen as a means to enlighten and liberate, serves the higher purpose of preparing minds and hearts for deeper communion.

In sum, the tradition of dialogue and cooperation has been a cornerstone of the Third Order Regular Franciscans' mission. It is a living testament to the transformative power of humility, love, and mutual respect. As the world becomes increasingly interconnected, the need for such dialogue is more pressing than ever. The Franciscans remain steadfast in their commitment to this sacred work, confident in the words of Christ that "Blessed are the pure in heart: for they shall see God" (Matt. 5:8). Through their efforts, they invite others to witness the divine tapestry of human community, woven beautifully through threads of faith and understanding.

Shared Initiatives

The spirit of ecumenism and interfaith dialogue, inherent in the mission of the Third Order Regular Franciscans, has borne witness to a multitude of shared initiatives over time. These endeavors manifest the compassionate ethos of St. Francis of Assisi, drawing on his vision of universal fraternity and communion with all creation. Rooted in the Gospel's call to love one's neighbor as oneself ("Matt. 22:39"), these shared initiatives form the cornerstone of a collective journey towards reconciliation, understanding, and peace.

Among the most notable of these endeavors is the collaboration with other Christian denominations. The Franciscans have actively pursued unity with fellow Christians, engaging in joint worship services, theological dialogues, and community service projects. The Order's commitment to the ecumenical movement is an enduring testament to its belief that, despite doctrinal differences, all Christians are united in their love for Christ and their service to humanity. The spirit of mutual respect and cooperation exemplified in these partnerships reflects the profound desire for the Body of Christ to be "one, even as we are one" (John 17:22).

Interreligious dialogue, too, has been a focal point of the Franciscans' outreach. This extends beyond merely theological discussions to encompass practical cooperation on issues of common concern, such as poverty, environmental stewardship, and social justice. Working alongside Muslim, Jewish, Hindu, Buddhist, and indigenous communities, the Franciscans seek to foster mutual understanding and respect. These interfaith initiatives underscore a shared commitment to safeguarding the dignity of all people and promoting the common good.

Educational programs have also been a significant component of these shared initiatives. The Third Order Regular Franciscans have established several interfaith academic forums and institutes, providing spaces for dialogue, learning, and mutual enrichment. These institutions not only cultivate a deeper understanding of different faith traditions but also inspire students and scholars to work towards a more harmonious and just world. Through these educational efforts, the Franciscans contribute to forming a new generation committed to the ideals of peace and interfaith solidarity.

One remarkable example of interfaith cooperation is the collaboration in humanitarian aid and community assistance. When disaster strikes or crises arise, the Franciscans often join forces with other religious groups to provide relief and support. This practical collaboration transcends theological boundaries, emphasizing the shared human experience and the collective responsibility to serve those in need. The local and global efforts in areas such as refugee aid, healthcare, and disaster relief demonstrate the tangible impact of these shared initiatives.

Moreover, these shared initiatives frequently take form in artistic and cultural exchanges. Franciscan-inspired art, music, and literature often serve as mediums to bridge cultural divides and foster mutual appreciation. Exhibitions, concerts, and literary events co-developed with artists from diverse religious backgrounds celebrate the rich tapestry of human creativity and spirituality. These cultural endeavors not only showcase the unique contributions of different traditions but also promote a sense of unity and shared heritage.

The Franciscans' shared initiatives are also realized in their environmental advocacy. Partnering with other faith-based organizations, they work towards ecological conservation and sustainability. This collaboration is deeply rooted in the Franciscan understanding of creation as a manifestation of God's love, calling for stewardship and care for our common home. Joint projects in reforestation, conservation, and education on environmental issues exemplify this commitment, reflecting the scriptural mandate to "replenish the earth, and subdue it" (Gen. 1:28).

Furthermore, these initiatives often extend to the realm of advocacy and social justice. Unified in their pursuit of justice and equality, the Franciscans engage with other religious and secular organizations to combat systemic injustice and promote human rights. This alliance is reflected in campaigns against human trafficking, efforts to end poverty, and initiatives to ensure equitable access to essential services. Through these partnerships, Franciscans not only amplify their impact but also embody the call to "let justice roll down like waters, and righteousness like an ever-flowing stream" (Amos 5:24).

Noteworthy are the peace-building efforts that have emerged from these interfaith collaborations. In regions marred by conflict and division, the Franciscans have worked tirelessly alongside interreligious councils and peace organizations. By creating avenues for dialogue and reconciliation, they help lay the foundation for enduring peace. These efforts are vital in regions where religious identity has been a source of division, demonstrating the power of faith to heal and unite rather than divide.

Equally important, these initiatives often focus on empowering marginalized and underserved communities. By pooling resources and expertise, Franciscan initiatives with other faith groups seek to uplift those in society who are most vulnerable. These efforts range from providing educational opportunities and vocational training to offering healthcare and legal assistance. Through this committed work, the shared initiatives strive to reflect the promise that "the meek shall inherit the earth" (Matt. 5:5).

The shared initiatives of the Third Order Regular Franciscans affirm a profound commitment to the vision of St. Francis of Assisi: a world where all, regardless of belief or background, are seen as brothers and sisters. These collaborative undertakings extend a hand of fellowship, striving to build bridges over the divides of religion, culture, and ideology. They model a way of coexistence rooted in love, respect, and a deep sense of shared humanity.

In essence, the shared initiatives of the Franciscans reveal a quest for unity that is both spiritual and practical. They illuminate a path where dialogue is not a mere formality but a transformational encounter, where cooperative efforts serve not only the immediate needs of communities but also the broader mission of creating a world imbued with the spirit of peace and brotherhood. By focusing on common goals and shared values, the Franciscans and their interfaith partners strive to create a legacy of justice, peace, and mutual respect for generations to come.

Chapter 23: Technology and Modern Evangelization

In an era where "the word of the Lord endureth forever" (1 Peter 1:25), the Franciscans have embraced contemporary technologies to breathe new life into their mission of evangelization. Utilizing digital platforms to spread the Gospel, the Third Order has adeptly woven modern communication tools into their spiritual fabric, channeling the ancient spirit of St. Francis into the pixels and bytes of today's interconnected world. From social media to podcasts, online masses to virtual retreats, these innovative methods serve as the new testament to their enduring commitment to spreading love and truth. Emulating the Apostles who "went forth, and preached everywhere" (Mark 16:20), the Franciscans now navigate the digital highways, ensuring their presence is not confined to physical boundaries but extends to the furthest reaches of cyberspace, touching hearts and kindling faith in unprecedented ways.

Digital Presence and Outreach

The realm of digital presence and outreach stands as both a challenge and an opportunity for the Third Order Regular Franciscans in an era marked by rapid technological advances. Embracing the digital domain allows the Order to expand its reach and share its message with a broader audience, going beyond the confines of cloistered walls and traditional mission territories. The words of the Savior command us, "Go ye into all the world, and preach the gospel to every creature" (Mark 16:15). The digital age provides new avenues to fulfill this divine mandate, enabling the Good News to be broadcast to the farthest corners of the earth.

The initial step in establishing a robust digital presence is the creation of well-constructed websites for the Order's various chapters, institutions, and initiatives. These websites serve as virtual portals through which visitors can learn about the Franciscan missions, upcoming events, opportunities for volunteerism, and the rich history and spirituality of the Third Order. The content must be thoughtfully curated to reflect Franciscan values — simplicity, humility, and devotion to God. Furthermore, aesthetically pleasing and functionally efficient websites become welcoming digital thresholds, reminiscent of the physical gates of ancient monasteries, inviting all who seek solace and knowledge.

Yet, a digital presence extends beyond websites. Social media platforms provide an expansive stage where the Franciscans can share daily reflections, scripture passages, and inspirational quotes, creating a continuous flow of spiritual nourishment. In the brevity of a tweet or the visual storytelling of Instagram, the timeless messages of peace, love, and brotherhood can captivate the hearts of modern audiences. Indeed, the simplicity of social media posts can convey profound truths, much like Jesus' parables, encapsulated in succinct yet powerful messages.

Moreover, online communities within these platforms can facilitate engaging dialogues among followers. These dialogues mirror the ancient gatherings of believers, sharing experiences and reflections, thus fostering a sense of unity among people scattered across diverse geographies. Private groups and forums can offer safe spaces where seekers and adherents alike can ask questions, seek guidance, and share testimonies. "Where two or three are gathered together in my name, there am I in the midst of them" (Matt. 18:20), declares our Lord. This promise holds true even in virtual assemblies, where His presence can be felt in the shared pursuit of spiritual growth.

In addition to social media, the production and dissemination of multimedia content, such as podcasts, webinars, and online retreats, can significantly enhance outreach efforts. Podcasts and webinars enable the Franciscans to discuss theological topics, share homilies, and conduct Bible studies, reaching individuals who might be unable to attend in-person gatherings. Online retreats and virtual prayer meetings offer solace and rejuvenation, particularly to those facing life's trials or confined by physical limitations. These digital offerings provide a sacred service, allowing the faithful to partake in communal worship and education from the comfort of their homes.

Educational initiatives find a potent ally in digital platforms. Online courses in Franciscan theology, history, and spirituality can inspire and educate a global audience. Collaborations with universities and seminaries to offer accredited programs further amplify the Order's educational outreach, ensuring that the rich Franciscan intellectual heritage is transmitted to future generations. By embracing e-learning platforms, the Franciscans continue their legacy as educators, adapting to modern modalities while preserving the integrity of their teachings.

Technology also facilitates the fundraising efforts necessary for sustaining charitable initiatives. Digital fundraising campaigns, integrated with social media and websites, have replaced many traditional methods, offering a convenient and immediate way for supporters to contribute. With transparency and accountability, these platforms enable donors to see the direct impact of their contributions, thereby fostering deeper connections between benefactors and beneficiaries.

The utilization of mobile applications can be transformative for daily spiritual practices. Apps offering daily prayers, meditations, and scripture readings can help individuals foster a consistent spiritual routine. Just as the monastic bells call the brethren to prayer, push notifications can serve as digital reminders to pause and reflect, integrating moments of devotion into the busyness of modern life. Applications designed for specific events, such as pilgrimage guides or conference apps, can enhance the experience by providing real-time information and facilitating community engagement.

The extension of the Third Order's digital footprint is not without its challenges. Building a coherent and disciplined online presence requires a concerted effort and resources. It demands discernment to ensure that the digital content remains faithful to Franciscan values and excludes the cacophony often associated with the digital world. The Franciscans must guard against the trivialization of sacred messages in the fast-paced scroll of social media, ensuring every post and interaction is imbued with reverence and purpose.

Moreover, success in the digital realm necessitates training members in digital literacy and content creation skills. Workshops and continuous learning opportunities can equip friars, nuns, and lay associates with the requisite competencies to navigate the complexities of the digital landscape.

Understanding cybersecurity, ethical digital practices, and staying abreast of technological trends are vital components of this modern apostolate. Just as Brother Elias of Cortona mastered the use of contemporary tools in his time, today's Franciscans must become adept in harnessing technology for the greater glory of God.

As the Third Order ventures deeper into the digital realm, collaboration with other religious orders and faith communities can foster comprehensive and enriching content. Joint initiatives for interfaith dialogue, online prayer vigils, and social justice campaigns can exemplify the Franciscan commitment to peace and brotherhood. By working together, diverse faith traditions can create a formidable online presence, promoting a message of unity and love in a fragmented world.

The digital presence of the Third Order also extends to maintaining an archive of its historical and contemporary contributions. Digital libraries and repositories can house vast collections of Franciscan writings, sermons, artwork, and educational materials. These resources provide invaluable access to scholars, theologians, and seekers worldwide, preserving the Order's rich heritage while making it accessible to future generations. The creation of interactive timelines and digital exhibitions can bring the Order's history to life, engaging audiences in an immersive exploration of its legacy.

As we advance in this journey toward a comprehensive digital presence, it is imperative to heed the counsel given to the early disciples: "Be ye therefore wise as serpents, and harmless as doves" (Matt. 10:16). The Franciscans are called to navigate the digital expanse with wisdom and humility, ensuring their outreach is guided by the Holy Spirit and rooted in Gospel values. Through this careful and prayerful approach, the digital realm can become a fertile vineyard, yielding abundant spiritual fruit for the glory of God and the service of humanity.

Innovations in Communication

The grace of God is manifold, and His servants have always sought to bring forth His word in ever more effective and far-reaching methodologies. It is written, "Go ye into all the world, and preach the gospel to every creature" (Mark 16:15). In our era, communication has evolved exponentially, and modern technology has furnished the Third Order Regular Franciscans with unprecedented tools to fulfill this divine commission. The fusion of timeless spiritual truths with contemporary innovations has enabled the Franciscan brotherhood to penetrate hearts and minds across the globe.

At the heart of these innovations lies the internet, a vast digital expanse that mirrors the boundless reach of the heavens. Through websites, blogs, and social media platforms, Third Order Franciscans disseminate their teachings, engage in dialogue with the faithful, and reach those yet to know the love of Christ. A simple post or tweet can travel the world in an instant, touching souls in far-flung lands. Truly, "the earth is the Lord's, and the fullness thereof; the world, and they that dwell therein" (Psalm 24:1), and now, His word can traverse this domain like never before.

One might ponder the profound impact of live-streaming and virtual gatherings. In the days of St. Francis of Assisi, a friar would traverse hamlets and cities, his voice limited by the distance he could travel. Today, a single live-streamed Mass or prayer service can unite thousands, if not millions, of believers who join in worship from their homes. These electronic sanctuaries foster a sense of community and continuity, aiding those who cannot attend physical gatherings due to distance, illness, or other barriers. The spirit of solidarity embraces them, affirming that "where two or three are gathered together in my name, there am I in the midst of them" (Matt. 18:20).

In addition to social media and live-streaming, podcasts and online courses have become sanctuaries of learning and reflection. Franciscan friars and sisters now have opportunities to produce and share extensive series on theology, spirituality, scriptural studies, and the Franciscan way of life. These digital classrooms transcend the confines of traditional education, inviting hearers into a deeper understanding of their faith at their own pace and convenience. The wisdom that pilgrims once journeyed miles to hear can now be accessed with a mere click, fostering a global fellowship of learners and disciples.

Moreover, mobile applications have emerged as a pivotal innovation in fostering regular spiritual practices. Numerous apps, created by and for Franciscans, offer daily reflections, prayer reminders, and scriptural readings directly to one's handheld device. The relentless pace of modern life often threatens to overshadow moments of prayer and contemplation. These tools serve as gentle nudges from the Holy Spirit, drawing believers back to the divine amidst their daily routines. As it is written, "pray without ceasing" (1 Thess. 5:17), and indeed, technology now helps to make this exhortation a practical reality.

The Franciscans' embrace of advanced technology extends even into realms such as virtual reality (VR) and augmented reality (AR). Imagine immersing oneself in a VR reenactment of St. Francis's life, experiencing his calling, his trials, and his triumphs. These empathetic experiences offer profound insights into the Franciscan charism, making history and spirituality vividly present and emotionally resonant. AR, similarly, enhances physical spaces—think of visiting a Franciscan site and, through one's smartphone, seeing historical annotations and stories of the saints who lived there. These innovations bring sacred history alive in ways previously unimaginable.

With the advent of blockchain technology, there are revolutionary new possibilities in ensuring the transparency and trustworthiness of charitable projects. Blockchain helps secure donation records and project funding paths, which can be a beacon of trustworthiness for modern donors wary of fraud. In this manner, the Franciscans maintain an unbroken line of integrity from St. Francis to today's benefactors, showcasing how "the righteous shall inherit the land, and dwell therein for ever" (Psalm 37:29), a land nurtured and preserved through faithful stewardship and transparency.

Email newsletters and online communities also play an essential role. They provide a steady stream of updates, spiritual encouragement, and calls to action to a worldwide audience of faithful. Unlike traditional mail, which can take weeks to reach its recipient, digital communication spans continents in seconds, enabling rapid responses and mutual support. Apostolic work, prayer requests, and community events can be organized and disseminated with unparalleled speed and efficiency. This immediacy echoes the scriptural imperative: "Behold, now is the accepted time; behold, now is the day of salvation" (2 Cor. 6:2).

Nonetheless, these innovations are not devoid of challenges. The digital world is replete with distractions and potential pitfalls. Maintaining a balanced, reverent online presence requires discernment and vigilance. The Franciscans must navigate this virtual landscape with the same wisdom with which Jesus sent His disciples: "Behold, I send you forth as sheep in the midst of wolves: be ye therefore wise as serpents, and harmless as doves" (Matt. 10:16). In the digital mission fields, the Franciscans' commitment to integrity and faith serves as a lighthouse, guiding both novices and seasoned believers through the tumultuous seas of the internet.

Furthermore, personal testimonies shared through blogs and videos often resonate deeply with those who yearn for authenticity. The Third Order Regular Franciscans narrate their encounters with God, the challenges of their apostolic missions, and the joys of communal life, thereby inspiring others to embark on their spiritual journeys. These stories reflect the timeless truth that "we are compassed about with so great a cloud of witnesses" (Heb. 12:1), and these witnesses, now digital, bear steadfast testament to the enduring power of faith.

In sum, the innovations in communication woven into the fabric of modern evangelization embody the Franciscan spirit's vitality and adaptability. As the world continues to embrace and evolve with technology, the Third Order Franciscans diligently harness these advancements, always ensuring that their core message remains rooted in Gospel truth and Franciscan simplicity. Their efforts amplify the timeless call to holiness and service, fulfilling Christ's mandate to "Go therefore and teach all nations" (Matt. 28:19). The echo of St. Francis's voice, blended with the gentle hum of digital transmissions, sings in unison to the glory of God, transcending time and space in the eternal mission of evangelization.

Chapter 24: Future of the Third Order

The Third Order Regular of St. Francis stands on the cusp of a transformative era, poised to navigate the intricacies of a rapidly evolving world while steadfastly upholding its sacred principles. The future beckons with both challenges and boundless opportunities for renewal in the spiritual vitality and social mission of the Order. As society pivots towards an ever more interconnected and digital existence, the need for a robust yet adaptive Franciscan presence becomes more paramount. In all endeavors, the Third Order aims to bridge the ancient wisdom of St. Francis with the fervor of youthful commitment, thereby ensuring its enduring legacy and relevance. "Behold, I make all things new" (Rev. 21:5), echoes the divine promise, invigorating a community that must constantly strive to cultivate holiness, compassion, and peace amidst the complexities of modernity.

Trends and Predictions

In the steady quill of time, the Third Order Regular of St. Francis has carved out a legacy both profound and enduring. As we look to the future, patterns emerge that paint a vivid picture of what lies ahead, illuminated by the enduring spirit and mission of this venerable order.

We begin by contemplating the evolving focus on environmental stewardship. In the tradition of St. Francis, who preached to the birds and revered all of God's creation, there is a burgeoning commitment to ecological initiatives. This reverence for the earth aligns with the growing global awareness of environmental issues. Many Third Order communities are leading efforts in sustainability, from adopting green practices in their daily lives to advocating for broader ecological reforms. This harmonizes with the scriptural call to be stewards of creation: "And God saw every thing that he had made, and, behold, it was very good" (Gen. 1:31).

In the realm of social justice, we see an invigorated dedication towards addressing modern inequalities and fostering systemic change. The Franciscan emphasis on poverty, humility, and service informs their approach to contemporary issues such as immigration, economic disparity, and racial injustice. This renewed focus is not just theoretical but deeply practical, manifesting in active ministries that provide tangible support to marginalized communities. This aligns with the Biblical mandate: "Defend the poor and fatherless: do justice to the afflicted and needy" (Ps. 82:3).

Youth engagement stands as another towering pillar of the Third Order's future. As the age-old traditions meet the vigor of youth, there is a dynamic interplay that promises growth and renewal. Younger generations are being drawn to the Franciscan way of life, inspired by its authentic spirituality and deep-rooted commitment to peace and justice. This infusion of youthful energy is essential for the order's vitality, providing new perspectives while ensuring the continuity of age-old wisdom. The leaders of tomorrow are forming today, engaging in both digital evangelization and community outreach to make faith accessible and relevant to their peers.

The digital age brings both challenges and opportunities for evangelization. The Third Order's embrace of modern communication tools signifies a strategic shift in how they spread their message of peace and goodwill. Social media, online courses, and virtual retreats are now integral to their outreach strategy, enabling them to reach a global audience in unprecedented ways. This evolution ensures their message resonates with a generation that lives and breathes digital connectivity. Evangelization today must also contend with competing secular ideologies, necessitating a robust and nuanced approach to faith communication.

Interfaith dialogue is another crucial trend. The Third Order, rooted in the universality of Christ's love, is increasingly engaging in conversations and partnerships with other faith traditions. This movement towards inclusivity fosters mutual understanding and cooperation, which are indispensable in a world frequently marred by division. Their efforts resonate with the exhortation, "Love your enemies, do good to them which hate you, bless them that curse you, and pray for them which despitefully use you" (Luke 6:27-28).

In the academic sphere, we anticipate a continued emphasis on educational initiatives that integrate faith and reason. The Franciscan University of Steubenville exemplifies this trend, offering robust academic programs that are firmly grounded in the Franciscan intellectual tradition. This approach prepares students not only with knowledge but with a moral compass that aligns with the Gospel truths. The integration of theological depth with practical disciplines is pivotal in shaping leaders who are both spiritually grounded and intellectually equipped.

Healthcare and social services continue to be vital areas of ministry for the Third Order. As healthcare needs evolve, especially in the wake of global health crises, the Third Order's commitment to compassionate care remains steadfast. They are adapting to contemporary challenges by incorporating holistic and integrative approaches to health, which consider both physical and spiritual well-being. This aligns with the healing ministry of Jesus, "And he healed many that were sick with divers diseases, and cast out many devils" (Mark 1:34).

We also foresee significant developments in the realm of theological contributions. The intellectual heritage of the Franciscans is robust, and future endeavors are likely to build on this foundation with new insights and writings that address contemporary spiritual and ethical questions. Scholars within the Third Order are poised to contribute to ongoing theological discourses, particularly those surrounding ecology, social justice, and interfaith relationships.

Political advocacy is becoming an increasingly important aspect of the Third Order's mission. Inspired by St. Francis's legacy of peace and reconciliation, they are taking active roles in advocating for policies that reflect Christian values of justice, mercy, and humility. This includes involvement in legislative processes, public discourse, and grassroots movements aimed at fostering social and environmental justice. The prophetic voice of the Franciscans will continue to be a clarion call for transformation in society.

Meanwhile, the Third Order's contributions to the arts and culture are likely to flourish, building on their rich heritage of artistic expression. Through literature, music, and visual arts, the Franciscans will continue to inspire and communicate profound spiritual truths, crafting works that resonate deeply with the human soul. Artistic expression remains a powerful medium for evangelization and spiritual enrichment, bridging the ancient and the modern in ways that words alone cannot.

Ecumenism will see new heights, as the Third Order seeks unity with other Christian denominations. Inspired by the prayer of Christ, "That they all may be one" (John 17:21), they are working towards greater cooperation with other Christian communities. This endeavor aims to foster unity in diversity, presenting a united front in the mission of love and service to the world.

The organizational structure of the Third Order may see reforms as they strive for greater flexibility and responsiveness to contemporary needs. Such reforms could include changes in governance, community living arrangements, and the formation processes to better support modern vocations. These adjustments will help the order maintain relevance and effectiveness in its mission.

Lastly, the ongoing dialogue with contemporary culture cannot be overstated. The Third Order is increasingly engaging with the cultural trends and technological advancements that shape modern life. Through discerning engagement, they seek to baptize the culture with the Gospel message, transforming it from within. This involves a delicate balance of upholding timeless truths while addressing the ever-changing landscape of human experience and societal norms.

In summary, the future of the Third Order is marked by a harmonious blend of tradition and innovation. Anchored in the enduring principles of St. Francis and inspired by the Holy Spirit, the Third Order will continue to shine forth as a beacon of hope, compassion, and truth in a world that desperately needs all three. Through environmental stewardship, social justice, youth engagement, digital evangelization, interfaith dialogue, academic excellence, healthcare compassion, theological contributions, political advocacy, artistic endeavors, ecumenism, organizational reforms, and cultural dialogue, the Third Order embraces a future that echoes the eternal call of the Gospel.

Youth Engagement

In the ever-evolving tapestry of the Third Order, the engagement of youth emerges as a vital strand. The vigor and passion of youth, akin to new wine in old wineskins, invigorate the Order with renewed purpose and vision. As we delve into the milieu of youth engagement, it is crucial to understand the spiritual and practical dimensions that undergird this endeavor. "Let no man despise thy youth; but be thou an example of the believers, in word, in conversation, in charity, in spirit, in faith, in purity" (1 Tim. 4:12).

The youthful become torchbearers of the Franciscan charism, where the legacy of St. Francis is enkindled in their hearts. They are called to live the Gospel in radical ways, echoing the simplicity and humility that characterized St. Francis himself. Their engagement begins with the inculcation of the Franciscan spiritual ethos, drawing from a wellspring of prayer, community, and service. It is here that the seeds of future leadership and devotion are planted, nourished by daily interactions and communal living.

One cannot overlook the manifold forms of service that young members undertake. From tending to the marginalized to environmental stewardship, their actions testify to a living faith. In the spirit of St. Francis, who saw Christ in the leper, today's youth are encouraged to see Christ in all, particularly those on the peripheries of society. Such engagement is not merely social activism; it is a profound expression of Catholic social teaching, where faith and works coalesce.

Educational initiatives play a pivotal role in youth engagement. The foundational teachings of Franciscan spirituality are imparted through programs and seminars, fostering an environment of holistic learning. Youth are taught to integrate their academic pursuits with spiritual growth, mirroring the synthesis of faith and reason. "And be not conformed to this world: but be ye transformed by the renewing of your mind" (Rom. 12:2). This transformative education equips them to navigate the complexities of the modern world while staying rooted in their faith.

Mentorship is another cornerstone of engaging the youth within the Third Order. Seasoned members provide guidance and support to younger brothers and sisters, creating a continuum of wisdom and experience. This intergenerational dialogue enriches the community, ensuring that the spiritual and practical knowledge accumulated over centuries is passed down effectively. It forms a living tradition, where old and new coexist harmoniously.

The community's liturgical life also offers profound opportunities for youth involvement. Participating in daily Mass, Vespers, and other liturgical celebrations, the young are woven into the very fabric of the community's prayer life. "I will bless the Lord at all times: his praise shall continually be in my mouth" (Ps. 34:1). Through music, readings, and active roles in the liturgy, they experience firsthand the beauty and solemnity of Catholic worship.

Modern technology has become an indispensable tool in reaching and engaging youth. Social media platforms, digital retreats, and online forums allow for a dynamic exchange of ideas and spiritual resources. These digital spaces provide a sense of connection and community, transcending geographical boundaries. They are fertile grounds for evangelization, where the message of St. Francis can be broadcast to a global audience.

Youth camps and retreats further enhance engagement by offering immersive experiences in Franciscan spirituality and community life. In these settings, young people encounter a tangible expression of the Third Order's charism. They are given the space to reflect, pray, and form bonds with peers who share similar values. These experiences often serve as catalysts for deeper commitment and discernment of one's vocation within the Order.

Art and creativity also play a significant role in youth engagement. The young are encouraged to explore their artistic talents within the framework of Franciscan spirituality, whether through music, visual arts, or writing. Their creative expressions become acts of glorifying God, resonant with the Franciscan appreciation for the beauty of creation. "Let everything that hath breath praise the Lord. Praise ye the Lord" (Ps. 150:6).

The engagement of youth in the Third Order is not without its challenges. Secular influences and the distractions of modern life can pose significant hurdles. Thus, the Order continually seeks innovative ways to make the Franciscan message relevant and appealing to young hearts and minds. This requires a delicate balance of fidelity to tradition and openness to new expressions of spirituality and community life.

In addressing these challenges, collaboration with other Franciscan Orders and Catholic organizations becomes essential. Joint initiatives and projects provide expanded platforms for youth engagement, pooling resources and expertise. Such collaborations reinforce the universality of the Franciscan mission and offer young people diverse avenues to live out their faith.

The future of the Third Order hinges on this dynamic engagement of its youth. Their infusion into the Order ensures its continuity and vitality, echoing the promise of renewal that pervades the Gospel. With each generation, the torch of Franciscan spirituality is passed on, enveloping new hearts in its transformative fire.

Ultimately, the engagement of youth is a testament to the enduring relevance and appeal of the Franciscan way of life. As they embark on this journey, these young men and women find themselves part of a grand narrative, one that transcends time and space. In their hands, the future of the Third Order gleams with hope and promise, a beacon of faith lighting the path for generations to come.

Chapter 25: Personal Stories and Testimonials

In the tapestry of the Third Order Regular Franciscans' rich history, the profound personal stories and testimonials of its lay and consecrated members shine as beacons of faith and devotion. Brother Stephen's transformative journey from a life of materialism to one of spiritual richness echoes the parable of the prodigal son, reminding us that "I say unto you, that likewise joy shall be in heaven over one sinner that repenteth" (Luke 15:7). Meanwhile, Sister Margaret's steadfast commitment to serving the destitute in urban areas exemplifies the Beatitudes, living out the call to "Blessed are the pure in heart: for they shall see God" (Matt. 5:8). These narratives, varied yet unified in purpose, provide a powerful testimony to the enduring impact of Franciscan spirituality. Each story is a testament to the transformative power of a life dedicated to God, illustrating that the divine grace which guided St. Francis still flows abundantly through the lives of the Third Order's members today.

Inspiring Life Stories

The Third Order Regular Franciscans have long been heralded as beacons of faith, embodying the spirit of St. Francis of Assisi in both word and deed. Through their unwavering commitment to Christ and to serving the community, their lives have become the very pages of spiritual edification and historical testimony. Throughout history, certain individuals have stood out, their stories not merely tales of personal triumph but epic narratives that illuminate the path for others in the service of the Lord.

A shining example is Servant of God, Mary Elizabeth Lange. Born in the late 18th century in Haiti, she eventually found her way to Baltimore, Maryland. There, amidst injustices and societal challenges, she felt a divine calling to educate African-American children. Undeterred by racial barriers, she founded the Oblate Sisters of Providence, the first Catholic sisterhood for women of African descent. Her story is not only an account of facing adversity but a testament to the Franciscan spirit of inclusivity and education. As the Psalmist writes, "Thy word is a lamp unto my feet, and a light unto my path" (Ps. 119:105). Indeed, Lange's life shone brightly in the darkest times, guiding others towards the light of God's love.

The life of Blessed Franz Jägerstätter, martyr of the Third Order, is another awe-inspiring tale. Amidst the horror and moral depravity of World War II, Franz chose the narrow path of resistance against the Axis powers. Born in a small Austrian village, this humble farmer refused to serve in Hitler's army, motivated by an unwavering Christian conscience and a deep Franciscan spirituality. Arrested and executed for his stance, his resolute faith and courage remain a powerful example of standing firm for righteousness. "He that endureth to the end shall be saved" (Matt. 10:22)—his martyrdom a solemn echo of this eternal truth.

Consider also the transformative work of Dorothy Day, an American laywoman who became a Third Order Franciscan after a tumultuous early life. A convert to Catholicism, Day co-founded the Catholic Worker Movement, which sought to emulate Christ's commandment by addressing social injustice. Through her tireless service to the poor and her advocacy for peace, Dorothy Day exemplified the very essence of the Franciscan call to poverty, humility, and acts of charity. "Blessed are the peacemakers: for they shall be called the children of God" (Matt. 5:9). Her journey from a life of worldly disillusionment to one of deep spiritual fulfillment provides an indelible guide for those navigating the complexities of modern-day faith.

Another fascinating figure is Fr. Mychal Judge, OFM, a chaplain for the New York City Fire Department. Father Mychal's ministry touched countless lives, attending to the spiritual needs of firefighters and their families. He perished in the 9/11 attacks while administering last rites to fallen firefighters. Renowned for his boundless compassion and unyielding commitment to the Franciscan way, his life and death underscore the sacrificial love at the heart of Christian service. "Greater love hath no man than this, that a man lay down his life for his friends" (John 15:13).

In China, the story of St. Joseph Zhang Dapeng embodies the trials and triumphs of early Franciscan missionaries in Asia. A convert to Catholicism and a merchant by trade, Zhang utilized his vocation to spread the Gospel. Despite hostility and eventual martyrdom, he remained steadfast in his faith. His sacrifice resonated, leading to the proliferation of Catholicism in the region. His life illuminates the Franciscan approach to evangelization, marked by personal sacrifice and steadfast witness to the faith.

Then there is the poignant tale of Blessed Angela of Foligno, whose life serves as a remarkable testament to the transformative power of divine grace. Born into a life of privilege, Angela led a worldly existence until a series of personal tragedies, including the loss of her husband and children, invoked a deep spiritual awakening. She chose to embrace a life of extreme penance and profound mystical contemplation. Angela's writings, rich with spiritual insights, continue to inspire theological reflection and devotion. Her journey exemplifies the Psalmist's cry: "Create in me a clean heart, O God; and renew a right spirit within me" (Ps. 51:10).

Let us not overlook Brother Juniper, whose story, though laced with humor, imparts deep spiritual lessons. An early companion of St. Francis, Brother Juniper embraced simplicity to extraordinary lengths. His zealous acts of charity, often seen as imprudent by contemporaries, were imbued with genuine humility and pure-heartedness. The tales of Brother Juniper, be they apocryphal or rooted in historical fact, serve as a delightful yet profound reminder of the childlike faith and joyful service advocated by St. Francis. "Whosoever therefore shall humble himself as this little child, the same is greatest in the kingdom of heaven" (Matt. 18:4).

The influence of Third Order Franciscans extends into the realms of the intellectually profound as well. St. Bonaventure, who joined the Franciscan Order and significantly shaped its theological framework, offers another narrative of inspiration. Known as the "Seraphic Doctor," his theological works harmonize faith and reason, bridging the mystical and scholastic traditions. His intellectual rigor and spiritual depth left an indelible mark on Christian doctrine, echoing the Apostle Paul's exhortation: "Study to shew thyself approved unto God, a workman that needeth not to be ashamed, rightly dividing the word of truth" (2 Tim. 2:15).

The lives of these illustrious members are not mere historical footnotes but living testimonies of grace in action. They present an enduring legacy that continues to inspire successive generations, urging them towards greater spiritual heights and deeper communal bonds. The narrative threads woven by these lives demonstrate a faith that is not static but dynamic, continuously adapting and eternally relevant.

This chapter on inspiring life stories isn't simply a memorial of past achievements. It serves as a guiding light, illuminating the virtues to be cultivated in our current spiritual journeys. Their stories, etched in the annals of the Third Order Regular Franciscans, testify to a vibrant faith and a transcendent hope. As we meditate on their lives, we are reminded of the ceaseless call to live out the Gospel with fervor and authenticity, mirroring the undying love of the saints who have gone before us. "Wherefore seeing we also are compassed about with so great a cloud of witnesses, let us lay aside every weight... and let us run with patience the race that is set before us" (Heb. 12:1).

Testimonials from Lay and Consecrated Members

Within the sacred folds of the Third Order Regular of Saint Francis, the voices of both lay and consecrated members create a tapestry of faith and spiritual resilience. These testimonials not only illuminate individual journeys but also highlight the shared mission that binds this diverse community in the light of Christ.

John, a devoted lay member, recounts his transformative journey into the Third Order, starting as a quest for deeper meaning in life. He speaks with heartfelt reverence about the moment he felt called to embrace the Franciscan path. "For I was an hungred, and ye gave me meat: I was thirsty, and ye gave me drink: I was a stranger, and ye took me in" (Matt. 25:35). John's words resonate with the generosity and compassion found in Christ's teachings, guiding him to serve with humility and love.

Meanwhile, Sister Maria, a consecrated nun, envisions her path as a commitment to undivided devotion. She describes her daily life, where prayer and service converge to create a rhythm of peace and fulfillment. Her reflections mirror the Psalmist's declaration, "The Lord is my shepherd; I shall not want" (Ps. 23:1). For Sister Maria, these words are not mere verses but a mandate to live in serenity and trust in God's providence.

Another lay member, Lucia, shares her challenging yet rewarding experience working in social justice initiatives. Her journey was ignited by a sermon she heard years ago, which planted a seed of relentless advocacy for the marginalized. "Blessed are the merciful: for they shall obtain mercy" (Matt. 5:7). Lucia's resolve is steadfast, turning faith into action as she navigates the complexities of modern-day social issues. Her dedication has inspired many within her community, making tangible the Biblical call to mercy.

Father Dominic, a seasoned friar, narrates his lifelong mission work in lands far from his birth. The spirit of evangelization is the core of his calling, fueled by the words of Christ, "Go ye into all the world, and preach the gospel to every creature" (Mark 16:15). His stories of hardship and hope, encountering both resistance and acceptance, paint a vivid picture of a servant unwavering in his commitment to spread the message of love and salvation.

Lay member Thomas speaks of his involvement in spiritual education, mirroring the timeless question of seeking and finding. His devotion to teaching young minds is anchored in the assurance, "Ask, and it shall be given you; seek, and ye shall find; knock, and it shall be opened unto you" (Matt. 7:7). By instilling these values in his students, Thomas perpetuates a cycle of wisdom and virtue, nurturing future generations in the faith.

Consecrated member Sister Agnes brings a different perspective, reflecting on the simplicity and joy of daily monastic life. Her siren call is found in the simple act of communal living, sharing life with others in mutual service and prayer. The words, "Behold, how good and how pleasant it is for brethren to dwell together in unity!" (Ps. 133:1), encapsulate her experience. Sister Agnes's tranquil demeanor and kind spirit are a testament to the beauty of a life lived in selfless harmony with others.

Elena, another lay member, explores the profound impact of combining career and vocation. As a healthcare professional, she embodies the Franciscan commitment to healing and caring for the sick and vulnerable. "Heal the sick, cleanse the lepers, raise the dead, cast out devils: freely ye have received, freely give" (Matt. 10:8). For Elena, each patient encounter is an opportunity to reflect Christ's love and compassion in her professional duties, making her work a living prayer.

Brother Mark, fulfilling his calling in the arts, blends creativity with spirituality, producing works that inspire and uplift. "Let every thing that hath breath praise the Lord. Praise ye the Lord" (Ps. 150:6). His artistry serves as a conduit for divine wonder, inviting others to see the beauty of God's creation. Brother Mark's pieces are more than just art; they are visual prayers that proclaim the glory of God in unique and profound ways.

Youthful lay member Sarah shares her fresh perspective, recounting her struggle to reconcile modern life's demands with her spiritual journey. Her words reflect a tension many young members face, yet she finds solace in Jesus' promise, "I am the way, the truth, and the life: no man cometh unto the Father, but by me" (John 14:6). Sarah's testimony speaks to the evolving nature of faith and the enduring relevance of ancient truths in contemporary contexts.

Consecrated member Brother Anthony, tasked with environmental stewardship, speaks passionately about his mission to care for God's creation. His inspiration comes from the Genesis account, "And God saw everything that he had made, and, behold, it was very good" (Gen. 1:31). Brother Anthony's stewardship efforts reflect a deep respect for the natural world, viewing environmental care as a sacred duty harmonious with Franciscan values.

Margaret, a lay member, offers insight into the joys and trials of community service. Her journey began with volunteering at a small parish outreach program, an endeavor that soon grew into a full-time ministry. "Inasmuch as ye have done it unto one of the least of these my brethren, ye have done it unto me" (Matt. 25:40). Margaret's story underscores the profound impact that even the smallest acts of kindness can have, reflecting the essence of Christ's teaching on service.

Father Lawrence's story delves into the contemplative aspect of the Franciscan life, underscoring the importance of silent prayer and meditation. "But thou, when thou prayest, enter into thy closet, and when thou hast shut thy door, pray to thy Father which is in secret" (Matt. 6:6). For Father Lawrence, these moments of solitude are vital to spiritual growth, providing clarity and renewal in a noisy world continually vying for attention.

Sister Sophia, who is dedicated to pastoral care, recounts her experiences providing spiritual support to those in crisis. Her work echoes the Good Shepherd's promise, "I am the good shepherd: the good shepherd giveth his life for the sheep" (John 10:11). Sister Sophia's comforting presence has been a lifeline for many, her gentle words and empathetic listening embodying the tender care of the Shepherd for His flock.

Finally, Brother Peter, whose ministry involves fostering interfaith dialogue, shares his commitment to building bridges of understanding. "Blessed are the peacemakers: for they shall be called the children of God" (Matt. 5:9). In a world often divided by faith and ideology, Brother Peter's tireless efforts bring people together, promoting unity in diversity and reinforcing the Franciscan commitment to peace and fraternity.

Each of these testimonials, whether from lay or consecrated members,

Conclusion

The journey of the Third Order Regular Franciscans, as traversed through the pages of this volume, is a tapestry woven with threads of devotion, sacrifice, and divine calling. From the humble beginnings inspired by St. Francis of Assisi to the profound global impact of their spiritual and temporal efforts, the narrative of the Third Order radiates with the light of Christ, reflecting the essence of the Gospel mission. Indeed, "For where your treasure is, there will your heart be also" (Luke 12:34).

The Third Order's foundation, rooted in St. Francis's vision, has blossomed into a movement that has profoundly shaped not only the Roman Catholic Church but the world at large. Their unwavering commitment to the Franciscan approach to Jesus, characterized by a simplicity and fervor that echoes the earliest days of Christianity, continues to inspire countless souls toward a deeper, more intimate relationship with the Divine.

Through the ages, these dedicated men and women have engaged in evangelization and missionary work, carrying the message of salvation to the farthest corners of the earth. They have established educational institutions that foster intellectual and spiritual growth, imbuing their students with both knowledge and the virtues of a Christ-centered life. The legacy of their contributions is a testament to their relentless pursuit of the Franciscan ideal.

Beyond the realm of the Church, the Third Order Regular Franciscans have left an indelible mark on society. Through social justice and charity work, they have uplifted the downtrodden and stood as beacons of hope for the marginalized. Their dedication to environmental stewardship embodies God's command to "replenish the earth, and subdue it" (Gen. 1:28), demonstrating a sacred duty to care for Creation as stewards, not owners.

Key figures such as St. Elizabeth of Hungary and Blessed Angela of Foligno have embodied the Franciscan spirit, their lives marked by extraordinary piety and service. Their sanctity and dedication resonate through history, reminding us that true greatness lies in humility and selfless love. The contributions of the Third Order are not merely historical; they are living, breathing testimonies of faith in action.

The Franciscan University of Steubenville stands as a contemporary beacon of this enduring legacy. Its mission, deeply rooted in the Franciscan tradition, underscores the transformative power of education infused with faith. The university's academic and spiritual contributions continue to shape minds and hearts, preparing students to be faithful witnesses in a complex, ever-evolving world.

In the gallery of saints, the Third Order boasts figures like St. Louis IX of France and St. Roch, whose legacies offer timeless examples of Christian virtue and service. Their lives, marked by a profound commitment to holiness and charity, serve as both inspiration and guideposts for those who seek to walk in their footsteps.

The theological contributions of the Third Order, encapsulated in key texts and the writings of luminary authors, are a treasure trove of spiritual wisdom and insight. These works, spanning centuries, offer a rich vein of thought that continues to inform and inspire theological discourse today.

Modern-day community life within the Third Order revolves around a vibrant structure and membership that navigates the challenges and opportunities of contemporary times. The adaptability and resilience of the Order allow it to remain relevant and impactful, continually drawing new members into its fold and nurturing their growth in accordance with Franciscan principles.

On the global stage, the Third Order's expansion to different continents and cultural adaptations illustrate the universal appeal and applicability of its mission. Despite diverse contexts, the core values and spirituality of the Order remain unchanged, reflecting the timeless nature of its foundational charism.

The artistic contributions of the Third Order—seen in architecture, literature, and music—are more than mere expressions of creativity. They are acts of worship and evangelization, communicating the beauty of the faith and the glory of God in forms that transcend time and space.

In personal spiritual practices and community involvement, the Third Order members exemplify the integration of faith into every aspect of life. Their engagement in both private devotion and public service affirms the holistic nature of Franciscan spirituality, which sees Christ in all things and all people.

Through prayer, both traditional and original, the Third Order maintains a direct line to the Divine. These prayers, echoing through the ages, are lifelines that sustain their mission and draw them closer to Christ. Hymns and songs, whether ancient or newly composed, lift their voices in praise and reflect the joy of a life dedicated to God.

Poems of devotion and reflection, similarly, offer profound meditations on the mysteries of faith and the experience of divine love. They remind us that the spiritual journey is as much about contemplation as it is about action, allowing for moments of introspection and connection with the Divine.

The relationship between the Third Order and other Franciscan Orders highlights a family dynamic built on collaboration and shared missions, each with distinctive roles that enrich the whole. This unity in diversity exemplifies the Body of Christ, where different parts work together in harmony, "fitly joined together and compacted by that which every joint supplieth" (Eph. 4:16).

The Order's educational contributions, particularly the founding of schools and universities, reveal a commitment to nurturing future generations in both faith and reason. Their pedagogical approaches, grounded in Franciscan values, create environments where students can flourish intellectually, morally, and spiritually.

Health care and social services provided by the Third Order reflect a tangible manifestation of the Gospel call to care for the sick and needy. Their hospitals, care homes, and social programs reach out to those in need, embodying Christ's compassion and mercy in very concrete ways.

Significant historical events, marked by milestones and challenges, have shaped the path of the Third Order. Overcoming obstacles and drawing strength from their faith, they have emerged resilient, continually renewed in their commitment to their mission. This resilience is a testament to the enduring power of their faith and the divine guidance that has led them through centuries.

The impact of Vatican II brought transformative changes to the Third Order, aligning it with contemporary practices while preserving its ancient spiritual heritage. This period of renewal has allowed the Order to engage more effectively with the modern world, continuing its mission with renewed vigor and relevance.

In the process of vocations and formation, the Third Order nurtures individuals, guiding them through a journey of deepening faith and service. This process ensures that each member is well-prepared to embrace the life of the Order fully, equipped with the spiritual and practical tools needed to live out their calling.

Ecumenical and interfaith efforts underscore the Order's commitment to dialogue and cooperation, breaking down barriers and building bridges of understanding and friendship. These initiatives reflect the inclusive spirit of St. Francis, who welcomed all people with open arms and a heart full of love.

In embracing technology and modern evangelization, the Third Order leverages digital platforms to spread the Gospel, reaching a wider audience and engaging with contemporary culture in innovative ways. Their online presence ensures that their message

Appendix A: Appendix

To bring forth the fullness and clarity of the Third Order Regular of St. Francis, this appendix encapsulates significant elements, punctuating pivotal aspects of their divine journey and earthly endeavors. Let it serve as both a reservoir of knowledge and a spiritual compass for those who seek to delve deeper into the sanctified and humanitarian chapters of the Third Order.

Key Dates and Milestones

The timeline of the Third Order Regular is dotted with sacred milestones and transformative events that have shaped its enduring legacy.

- **1212:** The formal establishment of the Third Order by St. Francis of Assisi, an inception of a divine mission.

- **1221:** The approval of the *Memoriale Propositi*, the foundational rule for the Third Order.

- **1289:** Pope Nicholas IV's confirmation of the Third Order with the *Supra Montem* bull.

- **1988:** The beatification of Blessed Angela of Foligno, a luminary in the annals of the Third Order.

Notable Figures

Among the numerous saints, blesseds, and notable members, the luminaries who have emblazoned the history of the Third Order Regular include:

- **St. Elizabeth of Hungary:** Exemplifying charity and humility, her life stands as a beacon of pious devotion.

- **Blessed Angela of Foligno:** Her mystical experiences and contemplative writings provide profound spiritual insights.

Biblical Foundations

The Third Order Regular has always drawn inspiration from the Holy Scriptures, weaving its teachings into the fabric of their daily lives. The scriptural exhortations such as "For even the Son of man came not to be ministered unto, but to minister, and to give his life a ransom for many" (Mark 10:45) and "Blessed are the peacemakers: for they shall be called the children of God"

(Matt. 5:9) resonate deeply within their commitment to service and peace.

Moreover, these Bible verses have served as the cornerstones upon which the virtues of humility, charity, and devotion are cultivated. The Third Order Regular's resilience through trials and tribulations has been consistently fortified by their faith.

Historical and Theological Texts

Throughout history, manifold texts have emerged, chronicling the theological underpinnings and practical embodiments of Franciscan spirituality. Several key texts that remain essential reading include:

- *The Little Flowers of St. Francis*

- *The Writings of St. Francis*

- *The Rule and Life of the Brothers and Sisters of the Third Order Regular of St. Francis*

Instruction for New Members

Understanding the process of formation and vocation is imperative for the sustenance and propagation of the Order. New members undergo a rigorous process of spiritual and practical training, as prescribed in the detailed guidelines and pastoral instructions.

The intricate steps, from initial discernment to solemn profession, mirror the journey of becoming fully entwined in the ethos of the Franciscan way of life. This spiritual path demands profound contemplation, dedication, and an unwavering commitment to the teachings of Christ and St. Francis.

Spiritual Practices and Prayer Life

Integral to the daily rhythm of the Third Order Regular are its spiritual practices, meticulously framed within the Order's constitutions. These devotional activities, ranging from communal prayer to Eucharistic adoration, ensure that members remain steadfast in their spiritual fervor.

Among the cherished prayers, the "Prayer of St. Francis" and the "Canticle of the Creatures" are particularly revered, reflecting the sanctified joy and humility that imbue the Franciscan tradition.

Concluding Remarks

As we bring this appendix to a close, let it be a testament to the enduring spirit of the Third Order Regular. Their unwavering journey, steeped in sacrifice and service, continues to inspire countless souls across the world. The confluence of their past, present, and hopeful future remains a bright light in the tapestry of Christian history and spirituality.

Glossary of Terms

This glossary serves as a sacred lexicon, elucidating the vital terminologies and expressions pivotal to understanding the hallowed journey and contributions of the Third Order Regular Franciscans. May these definitions illuminate the rich tapestry of faith, sacrifice, and devotion that this order embodies.

- **Advent:** The liturgical season characterized by the four weeks of preparation before the Nativity of our Lord.

- **Beatification:** A declaration by the Pope that a deceased person lived a holy life and is now "Blessed," which allows for limited veneration. It precedes canonization.

- **Canonization:** The act by which the Church formally declares a deceased person to be a saint, inscribing them in the canon of saints.

- **Charism:** A special spiritual gift or grace given by the Holy Spirit to an individual or community for the edification and service of the Church.

- **Consecrated Life:** A state of life recognized by the Church, characterized by the profession of the evangelical counsels of poverty, chastity, and obedience.

- **Evangelization:** The proclamation of the Good News of Jesus Christ through word and witness.

- **Friar:** A member of one of the mendicant religious orders, notably the Franciscans, characterized by a life of poverty, communal living, and active ministry.

- **Franciscan Rule:** The foundational guidelines and spiritual precepts established by St. Francis of Assisi for living a Gospel-centered life, adhered to by members of the Franciscan family.

- **Incarnation:** The Christian belief that the Word became flesh in the person of Jesus Christ (John 1:14).

- **Laudato Si':** An encyclical by Pope Francis reflecting on the care for our common home, highlighting the environmental stewardship cherished by Franciscans.

- **Liturgy:** The official public worship of the Church, including the celebration of the Eucharist and the Liturgy of the Hours.

- **Minor Friar:** Also known as Friars Minor, these are members of the Order founded by St. Francis of Assisi, highlighting their commitment to humility and service.

- **Penance:** Acts of repentance and reconciliation, a significant aspect of the Franciscan spiritual life, emphasizing conversion and renewal.

- **Portiuncula:** A small chapel in Assisi, Italy, highly revered by Franciscans as the cradle of the order and a place of profound grace and conversion.

- **Seraphic:** Referring to the Seraphim, the highest order of angels, often associated with St. Francis due to his vision of a Seraph bearing the marks of Christ's Passion.

- **Stigmata:** The mystical appearance of the wounds of Christ on a person's body, as experienced by St. Francis of Assisi.

- **Theotokos:** A Greek title for the Virgin Mary meaning "God-bearer," emphasizing her role in the incarnation of Jesus Christ.

- **Transitus:** The annual commemoration of St. Francis of Assisi's passing from this life to eternal glory on October 3rd, marked by solemn prayer and reflection.

- **Virtues:** The Firm and habitual dispositions to do good. Fundamental to Franciscan teaching are the theological virtues of faith, hope, and charity, and the cardinal virtues of prudence, justice, fortitude, and temperance.

For, 'Wherefore remember, that ye being in time past Gentiles in the flesh, who are called Uncircumcision by that which is called the Circumcision in the flesh made by hands;' so too, does this glossary guide your understanding (Eph. 2:11).

List of Important Dates

In the grand tapestry of history, the Third Order Regular Franciscans have woven many significant dates that mark their journey and contributions to the Church and the wider world. Documenting these moments not only honors their legacy but also serves as a beacon, illuminating the path of spirituality and service for future generations. From their founding to contemporary milestones, each date is a testament to their unwavering commitment to the Franciscan ideals of humility, charity, and devotion.

The origins of the Third Order Regular can be traced back to the early 13th century, during a time when St. Francis of Assisi felt divinely inspired to found a lay movement that would embody the virtues of simplicity and piety. It was in 1209, under the solemn skies of Assisi, that St. Francis received papal approval from Pope Innocent III to begin his mission, a date often regarded as the genesis of the broader Franciscan movement.

As the initial fervor of the Franciscan movement grew, St. Francis sought to extend his vision beyond the confines of the First and Second Orders. Thus, in 1221, he established the Third Order of Penance, which laid the groundwork for what would evolve into the Third Order Regular. This establishment provided a spiritual home for laypeople who desired to live out Franciscan principles without taking formal religious vows.

Another pivotal moment came in 1289 when Pope Nicholas IV, himself a Franciscan, promulgated the bull 'Supra Montem,' which offered a formal rule for the Third Order of Penance. This document solidified the ideals and practices of the Third Order, grounding its members in a life of penance, prayer, and charitable works.

The expansion of the Third Order Regular continued into the 15th century, marked by the approval of a more regulated and communal form of life for the Order by Pope Martin V in 1428. This period saw the Third Order Regular transition into a more structured organization, emphasizing community living and further distinguishing themselves from the secular branch of the Third Order.

Fast forward to more recent history, the Third Order Regular played an essential role during the reforms of the Second Vatican Council (1962-1965). Vatican II brought profound changes to religious life, encouraging a return to the original charisms of various Orders. The Third Order Regular embraced these reforms, which revitalized their mission and expanded their ministries to new pastoral and social settings.

In the light of modernity, the founding of the Franciscan University of Steubenville in 1946 became a landmark event, representing the Order's commitment to education and evangelization. This institution has grown into a beacon of Catholic higher education, deeply rooted in Franciscan values and dedicated to forming leaders who are fervent in faith and service.

Another cornerstone date in contemporary history is 1982, when Blessed Angela of Foligno, a notable member of the Third Order, was beatified by Pope John Paul II. Her life and writings continue to inspire many within the Order and serve as a profound example of mystical theology and divine intimacy.

Moreover, the canonization of St. Louis IX of France in 1297 by Pope Boniface VIII, who was a member of the Third Order, added a royal yet humble figure to the pantheon of Franciscan saints. His life as a king who served the poor and upheld justice exemplifies the Third Order's call to integrate faith with daily life and secular responsibilities.

In 1993, the Third Order Regular received new constitutions approved by the Congregation for Institutes of Consecrated Life and Societies of Apostolic Life, marking a significant evolutionary step in their governance and way of life. These constitutions reflect modern understanding while preserving the rich heritage and spiritual core of the Order.

The new millennium brought further recognition to the Third Order, with the beatification of more members who lived out their call to holiness within the scope of lay Franciscan life. The beatifications of Blessed Maria Plecia of Poland in 2002 and Blessed Ceferino Giménez Malla in 1997 symbolize the enduring relevance and sanctity found within the Third Order Regular.

The span from the 13th century to the 21st century is filled with these and numerous other dates that signify critical junctures and developments in the history of the Third Order Regular. Each date is not merely a point on a timeline but a narrative strand that adds to the rich, diverse, and sacred history of the Order. Rooted firmly in their Franciscan heritage, the Third Order Regular continues to adapt and respond to the needs of the time, staying true to their mission of living out the Gospel in simplicity and brotherhood.

Indeed, these important dates reflect a tradition that is both ancient and ever new, anchored in the timeless wisdom of St. Francis of Assisi and constantly renewed by the Spirit to meet contemporary challenges. The Franciscans remind us that history is not just a record of the past but a living guide that calls each generation to faithfulness, service, and love.

Notable Third Order Writings and Resources

The corpus of writings and resources associated with the Third Order Regular Franciscans is both rich and diverse, spanning centuries and encompassing numerous formats. These documents not only reflect the spiritual fervor and theological profundity of the order but also serve as indispensable guides for scholars, devotees, and practitioners alike. In essence, they mirror the journey of souls catching fire with divine love, echoing the wisdom handed down from St. Francis of Assisi himself.

Among the most esteemed writings, the "Rule and Life of the Brothers and Sisters of the Third Order Regular of St. Francis" stands paramount. This foundational text, amended and approved by various pontiffs over time, lays down essential guidelines for living a Franciscan lifestyle. The Rule exhorts its adherents to a life of penance, humility, and charity, rooted deeply in the evangelical counsels of poverty, chastity, and obedience. As it is written, "For even the Son of man came not to be ministered unto, but to minister, and to give his life a ransom for many" (Mark 10:45).

"The Admonitions" of St. Francis, a series of spiritual exhortations, also permeate the fabric of Third Order writings. These short, yet profound meditations capture the essence of

Franciscan spirituality - drawing the faithful towards a deeper understanding of humility, brotherly love, and reverence for God. In one of these poignant adages, St. Francis proclaims, "Blessed is the servant who would accept correction, accusation, and reproof from another as patiently as he would from himself" (Admonitions, XIII).

Reflecting the intellectual heritage of the Third Order, the treatises of Blessed Angela of Foligno offer a visionary and mystical dimension to their library. Her compilation, "The Book of Visions and Instructions," recounts a series of divine encounters and provides elucidations on profound theological complexities. Angela's texts are a testament to the spiritual depth achievable under the Franciscan mantle, revealing her intimate dialogs with the Divine.

Moving forward in time, the scholarly contributions of modern Franciscan theologians continue to fortify the theological framework of the Third Order. Works such as those penned by scholars like Father Zachary Hayes, OFM, unraveling the intricacies of Franciscan Christology, have been instrumental. In these volumes, readers are guided through a detailed exegesis of the Franciscan understanding of Christ - emphasizing the incarnational worldview, much as it aligns with the passage, "And the Word was made flesh, and dwelt among us" (John 1:14).

The Third Order's literary wealth isn't confined solely to theological treatises. Historical narratives, like the seminal "Chronicle of the Twenty-Four Generals," narrate the lives and virtuous exploits of the early Franciscan leaders, granting us a panoramic view of the Order's historical evolution. These chronicles, like beacons, illuminate the sacrifices and triumphs of those who carried forth the Franciscan mission - their tales akin to the apostles chronicled in "The Acts of the Apostles."

Another key resource is the "Manual of the Brothers and Sisters of the Third Order Regular of St. Francis," a comprehensive guide to the daily observances and liturgical practices tailored for the Third Order members. This manual isn't merely a directory of prayers but is rich with spiritual exercises, meditations, and practical guidelines aligned with living a Franciscan life. As Luke wrote, "And they continued stedfastly in the apostles' doctrine and fellowship, and in breaking of bread, and in prayers" (Acts 2:42), so does this manual serve to perpetuate such steadfast continuity in faith and practice.

Moreover, the poetic contributions of the Third Order must not be overlooked. From the venerated hymns of St. Bonaventure which exalt the majesty of God through his poetic liturgies, to the contemporary hymns that fill modern Franciscan convents and churches with melodic devotions, the lyrical compositions stand as testaments to the Franciscan artistic spirit. Drawing parallels to King David's psalmodic praises, "Make a joyful noise unto the Lord, all ye lands" (Psalm 100:1), these hymns continue to inspire and uplift the faithful.

Furthermore, the myriad biographies and hagiographies that detail the lives of Third Order saints, like St. Elizabeth of Hungary and St. Louis IX, offer invaluable insights into their spiritual journeys and saintly attributes. These texts, rich in narrative and inspirational depth, serve as guideposts for aspiring Franciscans and theologians, displaying the path of righteousness, charity, and unwavering faith. As Paul proclaimed in his epistle, "Wherefore seeing we also are compassed about with so great a cloud of witnesses, let us lay aside every weight" (Hebrews 12:1), these life accounts remind us that the Third Order's legacy is veiled in the sanctity of its predecessors.

Incontinuation, the digitization of many of these seminal texts has opened new avenues for global evangelization and catechesis. Initiatives like the Franciscan Digital Library have transformed the accessibility of these resources, making them available to a global audience. This digital repository houses texts, liturgical manuals, and scholarly articles, promoting deeper engagement with the Order's historical and theological heritage. As the psalmist sung, "Thy word is a lamp unto my feet, and a light unto my path" (Psalm 119:105), so does the digital age illuminate the path for contemporary and future Franciscans.

The inclusion of scholarly journals and academic theses further enriches the repository of Third Order resources. Publications in journals like the "Franciscan Studies" and doctoral dissertations on the Order's multifaceted impacts on theology, history, and social issues offer rigorous scholarly examination and critical analysis, indispensable for researchers and scholars. These works, much like Paul's letters, "prove all things; hold fast that which is good" (1 Thessalonians 5:21).

Beyond written texts, the oral traditions and teachings preserved through recorded sermons, conference speeches, and retreat reflections offer a dynamic and personal dimension to the Third Order's intellectual and spiritual treasury. These recordings capture the essence of lived Franciscan spirituality, resonating with the wisdom from the Proverbs, "Incline thine ear unto wisdom, and apply thine heart to understanding" (Proverbs 2:2). The voices of experienced Franciscans, imbued with the spirit of St. Francis, bring to life the ancient teachings in ways ever-relevant to contemporary contexts.

Lastly, the establishment of resource centers and educational institutions, such as the Franciscan Institute at St. Bonaventure University, underscores the Order's commitment to scholarly excellence and spiritual education. These institutions not only curate precious archival materials but also foster the formation of future Franciscan scholars and practitioners. The symbiotic relationship between the written word and its academic dissemination ensures that the spiritual and intellectual legacy of the Third Order endures across generations.

THE 15 PRAYERS OF ST. BRIDGET

These Prayers and these Promises have been copied from a book printed in Toulouse in 1740 and published by the P. Adrien Parvilliers of the Company of Jesus, Apostolic Missionary of the Holy Land, with approbation, permission and recommendation to distribute them.
Pope Pius IX took cognisance of these Prayers with the prologue; he approved them May 31, 1862, recognising them as true and for the good of souls.

As St. Bridget for a long time wanted to know the number of blows Our Lord received during His Passion, He one day appeared to her and said: "I received 5480 blows on My Body. If you wish to honour them in some way, say 15 Our Fathers and 15 Hail Marys with the following Prayers (which He taught her) for a whole year. When the year is up, you will have honoured each one of My Wounds."

He made the following promises to anyone who recited these Prayers for a whole year:

1. I will deliver 15 souls of his lineage from Purgatory.
2. 15 souls of his lineage will be confirmed and preserved in grace.
3. 15 sinners of his lineage will be converted.
4. Whoever recites these Prayers will attain the first degree of perfection.
5. 15 days before his death I will give him My Precious Body in order that he may escape eternal starvation; I will give him My Precious Blood to drink lest he thirst eternally.
6. 15 days before his death he will feel a deep contrition for all his sins and will have a perfect knowledge of them.
7. I will place before him the sign of My Victorious Cross for his help and defence against the attacks of his enemies.

8. Before his death I shall come with My Dearest Beloved Mother.
9. I shall graciously receive his soul, and will lead it into eternal joys.
10. And having led it there I shall give him a special draught from the fountain of My Deity, something I will not for those who have not recited My Prayers.
11. Let it be known that whoever may have been living in a state of mortal sin for 30 years, but who will recite devoutly, or have the intention to recite these Prayers, the Lord will forgive him all his sins.
12. I shall protect him from strong temptations.
13. I shall preserve and guard his 5 senses.
14. I shall preserve him from a sudden death.
15. His soul will be delivered from eternal death.
16. He will obtain all he asks for from God and the Blessed Virgin.
17. If he has lived all his life doing his own will and he is to die the next day, his life will be prolonged.
18. Every time one recites these Prayers he gains 100 days indulgence.
19. He is assured of being joined to the supreme Choir of Angels.
20. Whoever teaches these Prayers to another, will have continuous joy and merit which will endure eternally.
21. There where these Prayers are being said or will be said in the future God is present with His grace.

Each prayer is preceded by one Our Father and one Hail Mary.

Our Father, who art in heaven, hallowed be thy name.
Thy kingdom come.
Thy will be done on earth as it is in heaven.
Give us this day our daily bread and forgive us our

trespasses as we forgive those who trespass against us and lead us not into temptation but deliver us from evil. **Amen**

Hail Mary, full of grace, the Lord is with thee; blessed art thou among women and blessed is the fruit of thy womb, Jesus.
Holy Mary, Mother of God, pray for us sinners, now and at the hour of our death. **Amen.**

FIRST PRAYER
Our Father – Hail Mary.
O Jesus Christ! Eternal Sweetness to those who love Thee, joy surpassing all joy and all desire, Salvation and Hope of all sinners, Who hast proved that Thou hast no greater desire than to be among men, even assuming human nature at the fullness of time for the love of men, recall all the sufferings Thou hast endured from the instant of Thy conception, and especially during Thy Passion, as it was decreed and ordained from all eternity in the Divine plan.

Remember, O Lord, that during the Last Supper with Thy disciples, having washed their feet, Thou gavest them Thy Most Precious Body and Blood, and while at the same time thou didst sweetly console them, Thou didst foretell them Thy coming Passion.
Remember the sadness and bitterness which Thou didst experience in Thy Soul as Thou Thyself bore witness saying: "My Soul is sorrowful even unto death."

Remember all the fear, anguish and pain that Thou didst suffer in Thy delicate Body before the torment of the Crucifixion, when, after having prayed three times, bathed in a sweat of blood, Thou wast betrayed by Judas, Thy disciple, arrested by the people of a nation Thou hadst chosen and elevated, accused by false witnesses, unjustly judged by three judges during the flower of Thy youth and during the solemn Paschal season.

Remember that Thou wast despoiled of Thy garments and clothed in those of derision; that Thy Face and Eyes were veiled, that Thou wast buffeted, crowned with thorns, a reed placed in Thy Hands, that Thou was crushed with blows and overwhelmed with affronts and outrages.
In memory of all these pains and sufferings which Thou didst endure before Thy Passion on the Cross, grant me before my death true contrition, a sincere and entire confession, worthy satisfaction and the remission of all my sins. **Amen.**

SECOND PRAYER
Our Father - Hail Mary.
O Jesus! True liberty of angels, Paradise of delights, remember the horror and sadness which Thou didst endure when Thy enemies, like furious lions, surrounded Thee, and by thousands of insults, spits, blows, lacerations and other unheard-of-cruelties, tormented Thee at will.

In consideration of these torments and insulting words, I beseech Thee, O my Saviour, to deliver me from all my enemies, visible and invisible, and to bring me, under Thy protection, to the perfection of eternal salvation. **Amen.**

THIRD PRAYER
Our Father - Hail Mary.
O Jesus! Creator of Heaven and earth Whom nothing can encompass or limit, Thou Who dost enfold and hold all under Thy Loving power, remember the very bitter pain.

Thou didst suffer when the Jews nailed Thy Sacred Hands and Feet to the Cross by blow after blow with big blunt nails, and not finding Thee in a pitiable enough state to satisfy their rage, they enlarged Thy Wounds, and added pain to pain, and with indescribable cruelty stretched Thy Body on the Cross, pulled Thee from all sides, thus dislocating Thy Limbs.

I beg of Thee, O Jesus, by the memory of this most Loving suffering of the Cross, to grant me the grace to fear Thee and to Love Thee. **Amen.**

FOURTH PRAYER
Our Father - Hail Mary.
O Jesus! Heavenly Physician, raised aloft on the Cross to heal our wounds with Thine, remember the bruises which Thou didst suffer and the weakness of all Thy Members which were distended to such a degree that never was there pain like unto Thine.

From the crown of Thy Head to the Soles of Thy Feet there was not one spot on Thy Body that was not in torment, and yet, forgetting all Thy sufferings, Thou didst not cease to pray to Thy Heavenly Father for Thy enemies, saying: "Father forgive them for they know not what they do."

Through this great Mercy, and in memory of this suffering, grant that the remembrance of Thy Most Bitter Passion may effect in us a perfect contrition and the remission of all our sins. **Amen**.

FIFTH PRAYER
Our Father - Hail Mary.
O Jesus! Mirror of eternal splendour, remember the sadness which Thou experienced, when contemplating in the light of Thy Divinity the predestination of those who would be saved by the merits of Thy Sacred Passion.

Thou didst see at the same time, the great multitude of reprobates who would be damned for their sins, and Thou didst complain bitterly of those hopeless lost and unfortunate sinners.

Through this abyss of compassion and pity, and especially through the goodness which Thou displayed to the good thief when Thou saidst to him: "This day, thou shalt be with Me in Paradise." I beg of Thee, O Sweet Jesus, that at the hour of my death, Thou wilt show me mercy. **Amen**.

SIXTH PRAYER
Our Father - Hail Mary.
O Jesus! Beloved and most desirable King, remember the grief Thou didst suffer, when naked and like a common criminal.

Thou was fastened and raised on the Cross, when all Thy relatives and friends abandoned Thee, except Thy Beloved Mother, who remained close to Thee during Thy agony and whom Thou didst entrust to Thy faithful disciple when Thou saidst to Mary: "Woman, behold thy son!" and to St. John: "Son, behold thy Mother!"

I beg of Thee O my Saviour, by the sword of sorrow which pierced the soul of Thy holy Mother, to have compassion on me in all my affliction and tribulations, both corporal and spiritual, and to assist me in all my trials, and especially at the hour of my death. **Amen**.

SEVENTH PRAYER
Our Father - Hail Mary.
O Jesus! Inexhaustible Fountain of compassion, Who by a profound gesture of Love, said from the Cross: "I thirst!" suffered from the thirst for the salvation of the human race.

I beg of Thee O my Saviour, to inflame in our hearts the desire to tend toward perfection in all our acts; and to extinguish in us the concupiscence of the flesh and the ardor of worldly desires. **Amen**.

EIGHTH PRAYER
Our Father – Hail Mary.
O Jesus! Sweetness of hearts, delight of the spirit, by the bitterness of the vinegar and gall which Thou didst taste on the Cross for Love of us, grant us the grace to receive worthily.

Thy Precious Body and Blood during our life and at the hour of our death, that they may serve as a remedy and consolation for our souls. **Amen.**

NINTH PRAYER
Our Father – Hail Mary.
O Jesus! Royal virtue, joy of the mind, recall the pain Thou didst endure when, plunged in an ocean of bitterness at the approach of death, insulted, outraged by the Jews.

Thou didst cry out in a loud voice that Thou was abandoned by Thy Father, saying: "My God, My God, why hast Thou forsaken me?"

Through this anguish, I beg of Thee, O my Saviour, not to abandon me in the terrors and pains of my death. **Amen.**

TENTH PRAYER
Our Father – Hail Mary.
O Jesus! Who art the beginning and end of all things, life and virtue, remembers that for our sakes Thou was plunged in an abyss of suffering from the soles of Thy Feet to the crown of Thy Head.

In consideration of the enormity of Thy Wounds, teach me to keep, through pure love, Thy Commandments, whose way is wide and easy for those who love Thee. **Amen.**

ELEVENTH PRAYER
Our Father - Hail Mary.
O Jesus! Deep abyss of mercy, I beg of Thee, in memory of Thy Wounds which penetrated to the very marrow of Thy Bones and to the depth of Thy being, to draw me, a miserable sinner, overwhelmed by my offenses, away from sin and to hide me from Thy Face justly irritated against me, hide me in Thy wounds, until Thy anger and just indignation shall have passed away. **Amen.**

TWELFTH PRAYER
Our Father - Hail Mary.
O Jesus! Mirror of Truth, symbol of unity, bond of charity, remember the multitude of wounds with which Thou wast afflicted from head to foot, torn and reddened by the spilling of Thy adorable Blood. O great and universal pain, which Thou didst suffer in Thy virginal flesh for love of us! Sweetest Jesus! What is there that Thou couldst have done for us which Thou has not done!

May the fruit of Thy suffering be renewed in my soul by the faithful remembrance of Thy Passion, and may Thy love increase in my heart each day, until I see Thee in eternity: Thou Who art the treasure of every real good and every joy, which I beg Thee to grant me, O Sweetest Jesus, in heaven. **Amen.**

THIRTEENTH PRAYER
Our Father - Hail Mary.
O Jesus! Strong Lion, Immortal and Invincible King, remember the pain which Thou didst endure when all Thy strength, both moral and physical, was entirely exhausted, Thou didst bow Thy Head, saying: "It is consummated!"

Through this anguish and grief, I beg of Thee Lord Jesus, to

have mercy on me at the hour of my death when my mind
will be greatly troubled and my soul will be in
anguish. **Amen.**

FOURTEENTH PRAYER
Our Father - Hail Mary.
O Jesus! Only Son of the Father, Splendour and Figure of His
Substance, remember the simple and humble
recommendation.

Thou didst make of Thy Soul to Thy Eternal Father, saying:
"Father, into Thy Hands I commend My Spirit!" And with Thy
Body all torn, and Thy Heart Broken, and the bowels of
Thy Mercy open to redeem us, Thou didst Expire.

By this Precious Death, I beg of Thee O King of Saints,
comfort me and help me to resist the devil, the flesh and the
world, so that being dead to the world I may live for Thee
alone.

I beg of Thee at the hour of my death to receive me, a
pilgrim and an exile returning to Thee. **Amen.**

FIFTEENTH PRAYER
Our Father - Hail Mary.
O Jesus! True and fruitful Vine! Remember the abundant
outpouring of Blood which Thou didst so generously shed
from Thy Sacred Body as juice from grapes in a wine press.

From Thy Side, pierced with a lance by a soldier, blood and
water issued forth until there was not left in Thy Body a
single drop, and finally, like a bundle of myrrh lifted to the
top of the Cross Thy delicate Flesh was destroyed, the very
Substance of Thy Body withered, and the Marrow of Thy
Bones dried up.

Through this bitter Passion and through the outpouring of Thy Precious Blood, I beg of Thee, O Sweet Jesus, to receive my soul when I am in my death agony. **Amen.**

CONCLUSION
O Sweet Jesus! Pierce my heart so that my tears of penitence and love will be my bread day and night; may I be converted entirely to Thee, may my heart be Thy perpetual habitation, may my conversation be pleasing to Thee, and may the end of my life be so praiseworthy that I may merit Heaven and there with Thy saints, praise Thee forever. **Amen.**